YOU ARE YOUR CHOICES

ALSO BY ALEXANDRA STODDARD

Time Alive

Things I Want My Daughters to Know

Choosing Happiness

Feeling at Home

Open Your Eyes

The Decoration of Houses

Living in Love

Gracious Living in a New World

Mothers: A Celebration

The Art of the Possible

Alexandra Stoddard's Tea Celebrations

Alexandra Stoddard's Book of Days

Making Choices

Grace Notes

Creating a Beautiful Home

Daring to Be Yourself

Gift of a Letter

Alexandra Stoddard's Book of Color

Alexandra Stoddard's Living Beautifully Together

Living a Beautiful Life

The Postcard as Art

Reflections on Beauty

A Child's Place

Style for Living

You Are Your Choices

❋

50 Ways to Live the Good Life

Alexandra Stoddard

Collins
An Imprint of HarperCollins*Publishers*

HarperCollins books may be purchased for educational, business, or sales promotional use. For information please write: Special Markets Department, HarperCollins Publishers, 10 East 53rd Street, New York, NY 10022.

FIRST EDITION

Designed by Leah Carlson-Stanisic

✳ ✳

Library of Congress Cataloging-in-Publication Data

Stoddard, Alexandra.
 You are your choices: 50 ways to live the good life/Alexandra Stoddard.—1st ed.
  p. cm.
 ISBN: 978-0-06-089783-3
 ISBN-10: 0-06-089783-X
 1. Conduct of life. I. Title.

BJ1521.S84 2007
170'.44—dc22
                                                            2006049040
✳ ✳

 07 08 09 10 ID/RRD 10 9 8 7 6 5 4

TO MY THREE PRECIOUS GRANDCHILDREN:

All my love to Nicholas, Anna, and Lily

BIG MOMMY

The choice of a certain way of life . . . demands from the individual
a total change of lifestyle, a conversion of one's entire being, and ultimately
a certain desire to be and live in a certain way.

PIERRE HODOT

Contents

On the twentieth anniversary of Living a Beautiful Life
*and my twenty-fifth publication, I especially honor Carl Brandt
and Toni Sciarra. You have been and continue to be invaluable to my
inspiration as a writer. You have my deepest appreciation and love.*

An Invitation

This is an invitation to you to live the good life. In 1986, my fifth published book, *Living a Beautiful Life: 500 Ways to Add Elegance, Order, Beauty, and Joy to Every Day of Your Life*, was published. This book was about eating, sleeping, and bathing, and all the little ceremonies, celebrations, and rituals we can create in our daily lives to make us happier, healthier, and more fulfilled and to live more beautifully. That was twenty years ago. The experience of writing that book and the response from readers profoundly changed my life.

I'm humbled and grateful to learn from readers what a powerful impact this one book has had on their lives. And, while I've written twenty books since then, *Living a Beautiful Life* seems to be a favorite of so many of my readers. In it I introduced the concept of grace notes—little things we can do to make life more beautiful, more enjoyable, and more meaningful. When a publisher later asked me to write an entire book of grace notes, I leapt at the idea and ended up writing a book of meditations—grace notes for our mind, heart, and soul.

Living a Beautiful Life is a contemporary philosophy, a way of dignifying our lives, of turning the ordinary, routine things we all do each day into mindful acts of tenderness and love. When we set a pretty table, we are adding sweetness to the pleasure of a meal. By paying careful attention to all the common things, we elevate our lives in every area, and, as a result, we find great happiness in what we're doing. It makes perfect sense to find ways to take pleasure in the things we do every day.

Whenever we try to do things beautifully, we feel good about ourselves and make others feel good as well. Over the past two decades, I've met hundreds of people who have become friends—some close friends—because of this one book. Now it's time to expand and fulfill this basic philosophy. To live a beautiful life is our choice. I feel strongly that when we take care of the little things—the necessary and various parts—the big things, the whole of our lives, have greater significance and will be lived with more grace, love, and happiness.

The next step I invite you to take is *You Are Your Choices: 50 Ways to Live the Good Life*. I encourage you to read these fifty essays in any order you choose—just dive in and muse. The good life has no boundaries, only opportunities. Have fun. You are your choices. No one can put good thoughts in your mind but you. This book will challenge you. I urge you to join me on this quest. We'll keep evolving as we stretch ourselves to bring out the best that's inside us. We'll train our minds to think for ourselves.

Through study and concentration I've become convinced there is only one right way to live this brief life. To live well, we should choose to think wisely and do what is right, appropriate, and true. When we agree to accept this invitation to live the good life, we will honor our lives by pursuing our own personal happiness as we help others toward this goal.

The ancient Greek philosopher Aristotle has influenced my thinking. He has expanded my consciousness so that I am aware and understand that not only is happiness the aim and purpose of life for all human beings, but the way we achieve this goal is through the choices each of us makes. Aristotle admits this personal responsibility is tough: "Virtue, like art, constantly deals with what is hard to do, and the harder the task, the better the success."

Ask yourself, "How can I live the good life?" If this is your choice, you will pay closer attention to everything you choose to do as well as what you decide to give up or let go. The way things were is not the way things are. We are living in a world that demands our minds expand to greater awareness of reality. Aristotle teaches us about the Golden Triangle of the true, good, and beautiful. He points out there are right choices and wrong choices. The good life demands that we make the right choices most of the time, no matter how difficult they may be. The bad choice will not lead us to the good life. The good life is not only well lived but is the ideal that is pleasant and happy. As we examine how we can acquire all the things that are good for us and for others, we'll try to achieve more balance in our daily lives.

Say yes to this exploration of how to live more intelligently, with greater excellence and satisfaction. Do accept this invitation and we will be on our way.

Alexandra Stoddard

Stonington Village, Connecticut

Every Day, Commit Yourself to Experiencing the Good Life

I have never looked upon ease and happiness as ends
in themselves...The ideals that have lighted my way, and
time after time have given me new courage to face life
cheerfully, have been Kindness, Beauty, and Truth.

ALBERT EINSTEIN

In the twenty years since *Living a Beautiful Life: 500 Ways to Add Elegance, Order, Beauty, and Joy to Every Day of Your Life* was published, the greatest mind I have continuously studied for inspiration and insight is Aristotle. Born in Greece twenty-five centuries ago, this brilliant ancient philosopher has taught me more than any other thinker. We owe a huge debt to Aristotle's teachings. They have had a profound influence on Western thought. His philosophical system of empirical observation, logic, and uncommon common sense, his rational inquiry into the right way to live, ring true today. His ideas are as practical as they are wise.

Aristotle was a student of Plato, who, in turn was a pupil of Socrates. These illustrious giant thinkers disagreed on many issues, but they all believed that it is not simply *life* that we should value, but rather the *good life*. Later, Seneca, the ancient Roman stoic philosopher and writer, agreed with Socrates, Plato, and Aristotle that "to live is not a blessing, but to live well."

Many of my favorite thinkers have been led to the belief that the good life is the only life worth living. Ever since I went on a trip around the world in 1959, I've been on a quest to learn the ideals of as many great minds from the past as possible. I intuitively sensed that life is to be savored and should be lived accordingly. I read the works of the sixteenth-century French essayist Montaigne, I read Tolstoy, the Buddha, and the nineteenth-century thinker Emerson, along with dozens of others. I read Albert Einstein—one of the greatest minds of our time. His words leapt off the page one day and my heart pounded in joy. "Life is sacred, that is to say, it is the supreme value to which all other values are subordinate." Einstein picked up many of the threads of Aristotle's teachings. Aristotle believed we should live by the Golden Triangle of what is true, good, and beautiful. When we grasp what is true and good, we elevate our lives to become beautiful.

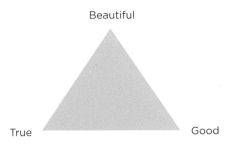

great minds from the past as possible. I intuitively sensed that life is to be

When we commit ourselves to live by these challenging three words — true, good, and beautiful—we transform our lives, because what is true, good, and beautiful represents universal values worth living for.

What is the good life? It is the life well lived, the happy life. Aristotle believed in and taught the virtues of happiness as the aim and goal of life; everything else was a means to an end. Happiness is the end. The good life is a life of moral excellence that leads to happiness. I've come to share Aristotle's deep conviction that there is only one right way to live for all people. Because we are all human beings, we all have the same basic needs and share common traits. To make a serious commitment to live a good life, with no time outs and no excuses, is a demanding discipline. Aristotle confesses that for any of us to live well is not easy.

We should not take life for granted for a minute, but far too many people take their entire lives for granted. As a result, they expect too little from themselves. Many people don't feel they deserve to be happy. We have to be hungry and thirsty for life abundant in order to fulfill our highest aspirations day to day. While some people just want to get by, we should choose to thrive. Coping isn't nearly as meaningful as thriving. We have to have a vision of unconditional love in order to become more loving. We have to have an understanding of contentment and happiness in order to achieve inner peace.

Who do you know and admire who lives his or her life well? How many of your family members and friends come to mind? There are educated, professional people who are not living the good life. We must all try to be more well rounded, to have more fun, to take more pleasure in the work we choose to do. There are certain things we must do to care for our basic needs. We need to train ourselves to take greater pleasure in whatever it is we're doing.

We should laugh more easily, smile more often, and be more cheerful. Life—to the wise—is not a burden to endure, but a precious blessing, a challenging adventure, to grow through. The opportunity to live well is a privilege. Wise Benjamin Franklin said that the noblest question in the world is "What good may I do in it?" Each natural catastrophe, every painful experience, all the terror and horror, are times to reach out to others with all of our inner resources—our compassion, empathy, love, and generosity. There is always good in bad situations. We can train our minds to see the good and to do good in the darkest moments of our lives.

What is the good life? The good life is a happy life because when we are happy, we will be good. We will do good for others when we have found our own happiness. Good is good through and through. Good is necessary in the little things we think and do, and in the big things we try to accomplish.

Aristotle doesn't let us off the hook. He believes we have an obligation, a duty, to live as beautifully and as humanly possible. This means to obtain and possess, over our entire lifetime, all the things that are good for us. The good life for yourself should be your ultimate goal that should influence all of your practical thinking, your choices, and your actions.

You are unique. You ought to do what no others can do, fulfilling your needs in vastly different ways. Your destiny is not predestined. You create your destiny every day, not by chance, but by choice. Destiny is an achievement. The power to achieve it is in your choices. You have a responsibility to dignify your life through continuously making yourself better. You should aim high for the good of all. I agree that there are forces beyond our control, but we are never in a choice-less moment to do the best we can.

When we're receptive to personal growth, to our ever-increasing, unfolding happiness, we are on our way, aiming our energies in the right direction. We're all capable of doing more good. Dare to live the good life now, right where you are, right in the good or bad situation you may be in. Affirm and reaffirm life by taking the high road. Devote yourself to life in all its manifestations, to raise it up to all its true glory. As thinking, feeling, loving beings, when we live up to our highest ideals and aspirations, we will be fulfilling our purpose.

Aristotle tells us we should try to develop a master plan for our lives. Socrates taught his students, "An unexamined life is not worth living." Aristotle agreed and added, "An unplanned life is not worth examining." Unless we have a plan for our lives, we won't know what we are trying to accomplish; we won't have a map guiding us to know where we're trying to go or how to get there. Another key is to have the right plan. This requires our being thoughtful, thinking through what goals we have, and how we can go about achieving them. When we have a good plan, we tend not to spin our wheels. Our life will add up to something that is satisfying, productive, and happy when it has structure and discipline.

A well-lived life is not an accident. The challenges some of us will face in the future are unprecedented. We must be prepared. We are not saints. We're often tempted. We will not always make wise choices, and we will have to live with the consequences and hardships as a result.

Nonetheless, we can recommit ourselves to the true, good, and beautiful. Never mistake your choice to live a good life for selfishness. This is what all of us ought to be choosing. By having a proper framework for right thinking and right action, we come to understand that we have a right to pursue personal happiness.

Life is a continuous progression in drawing from us our great potential. Ever unfolding, ever expanding, the good life is a big life that is rich, deep, and throbbing with opportunities to learn, to grow, to study, to teach, and to create. We have to stretch our imaginations to think fresh, new thoughts. We have to continue to be idealists, living by honorable and worthy principles. Practice envisioning things in their ideal form. Look for the greatest good all around you and inside you. Then, patiently pursue these great, noble ideals by your thoughtful choices. The people I most admire strive to do the right thing no matter how difficult or risky. Our choices should lead us to greater self-transformation.

Aristotle teaches us about the Golden Mean—the balance, the moderate position, between too little and too much. Be honest with yourself and learn the difference between your needs and your wants. All of our real needs are good for us. Many of our desires are also good for us, even though they may not be essential. We need food in order to survive. We may desire to have a truffle shaving or two on our salad or pasta, but truffles are not needed—they are, in moderation, for some of us, desired. By using the Golden Mean to poise ourselves between the two extremes of excess or lack, we're able to achieve an ideal balance.

We're here by chance or by amazing grace, not by our choice. Here we are. We can choose to be our best selves and to become all we're capable of becoming. When we dedicate ourselves to the practice of the good life, we approach our challenges with greater equilibrium and have a more positive, constructive attitude as we pursue excellence.

Trying to live well is not easy for any of us.

ARISTOTLE

2

Be True to All Your Choices

Choose well.

HOMER

When we make a serious commitment to live a good life, we have to be mindful and truthful in all our choices. Our choices should be consistent with reality. It is not easy to always make the right choice, but we should put everything into perspective, weigh the situation from all different angles, make a well-informed choice, and not second-guess ourselves.

So many people have a terrible time making up their minds. Indecision drains energy, causes procrastination, and keeps us from moving forward with life. We become scattered and confused. There is no absolute certain choice. There is only the wise, good choice at the time. My editor Toni Sciarra's father often said, "If you wait until you have all the information to make a decision, there's no decision to be made." Choice by definition contains ambiguity. But once you make a choice, you are free to change it under changed circumstances or in light of new knowledge. Perhaps you married the wrong person for all the wrong reasons when you were too young and immature, or you took on a business partner you later learned was corrupt. Say yes to the best choice while remaining flexible. Stay attuned to whether your choice continues to be appropriate and in your best interest. There are some irrevocable choices; you can't undo every choice. All the more reason to choose well.

You are your choices. You and I have the power, the right, and the freedom to choose for ourselves how to best live our lives. It is here, in our choices, that we build our character and moral goodness. We will make mistakes. But when we do, I believe it is noble to admit we were wrong, that we judged incorrectly, and need to reconsider our choice. No one will ever fully understand your choices. It's not other people's business to know the inner workings of your life, your marriage, your health, your finances, and your relationships. All you can do is be true to yourself in all your choosing. There is never a choice-less moment. If you genuinely try to make the best choice possible, the one that is in agreement with all the available facts, you will feel good knowing you are acting responsibly. You may have to choose to do something that you don't want to do, but you do it because it is the right thing to do.

Our power and strength lie in our ability to discipline our passions, to react in the right manner as we meet circumstances head on. You are choosing your ideal way of life, breath by breath, choice by choice.

We sometimes have to make tough choices that will improve a relationship or our finances or our health. Return to the Golden Mean for inspiration. Go to your center. Search your soul for guidance. Yes, you might need the money, but if the woman who offers you a job is rude, crude, and dishonest, you have to weigh the danger of having the job cost you too much. You could have good income but lose your soul's integrity.

Even good news often has some disadvantage that has to be weighed. You may get a wonderful job opportunity that would require uprooting your whole family and moving to a different state or force you to leave them for weeks at a time as you travel all over the world. What about your spouse and children? Don't you have to be true to your word to be there for them physically, emotionally, and spiritually, as well as financially?

The practical wisdom of the Golden Mean helps us to weigh every situation more realistically. The first principle is to do good. Identify the greater good and know that the good deserves to be pursued.

The great philosopher and author, and my friend, Dr. René Dubos taught Peter and me that people make choices based on what they want to be, to do, and to become. The way we evolve and transform ourselves is through our choices. "Choose well," and be true to all your good choices.

Life is the sum of all your choices.

ALBERT CAMUS

Be Responsible—Say No

> The world is full of people that have stopped listening to themselves or have listened only to their neighbors to learn what they ought to do, how they ought to behave, and what the values are that they should be living for.
>
> **JOSEPH CAMPBELL**

We sometimes forget that saying "No!" is a choice. Many decent, intelligent people have difficulty saying no to others' requests or demands. I've learned the power of no. I know how to make tough choices. In my New York office, on a stand on my desk next to the telephone, I keep a shiny fuchsia postcard with large block letters in white—NO. If I'm in the middle of a project that requires concentration, NO could mean I don't answer the telephone, preferring to listen to the answering machine when I'm free. NO could be to turn down a decorating project because my plate is too full. NO could be not to think negative thoughts, which cause mental confusion and sadness. There are great benefits to NO. We have to get over the embarrassment of being honest with others, afraid we'll hurt their feelings. No one else will ever know our circumstances or why we make the choices we do. Frankly, in most cases, it is none of their business. This is our life and we have to answer to ourselves, choice by choice.

Last summer a journalist from the *New York Times* called me to inquire about "The Five-Hour Rule" I wrote about in *Things I Want My Daughters to Know*. He was writing a column on the etiquette of houseguests. "What do you do when someone invites himself for the weekend?" "What do you do when you invite a friend who asks you if he can bring a friend, someone you've never met?" "How do you invite someone for just one night, not the whole weekend?" I laughed and said, "Say NO." I explained I was writing a book and houseguests are not an option. "But what about the times when you're not writing a book under deadline, and you have to make these decisions?" I again laughed and said, "I'd write another book."

Peace of mind is fundamental to living the good life. Our ability to say no is a major factor in our subjective well-being and our sense of satisfaction. Use NO as your teacher. Don't you usually know what feels right for you? Until you exercise your power to be honest with yourself and others, you are going to feel trapped, believing you have little control over your destiny. But you can make the choice to do what is right for you. You can't go through life "making an effort," time after time, and not doing what is right for you.

Emerson wrote in his journal that he likes the "sayers of NO" better than the "sayers of YES." When you are faced, point blank, with a spontaneous choice, it is your choice to make it crisply, clearly, and immediately. Nip things in the bud.

Leonardo da Vinci's wisdom is helpful to us in our decisions: "It is easier to resist at the beginning than at the end." If you aren't able to say NO right up front, you end up becoming reluctantly involved. Then you have to back off awkwardly and painfully. Once I let people show me the blueprints and photographs of their house and a file folder full of the things they like, I'm involved. A crisp NO wastes no one's time, energy, or money.

A publisher visited my husband, Peter, in his office several years ago and asked him if he'd be interested in writing a definitive book about the history of the law profession in America. This book, Peter was told, would be a ten-year project and require hiring researchers. Peter clearly knew this was not how he wanted to spend the last decade or so of his legal career or his life. He did not say, "Let me think about it." He said NO.

"Every great mistake has a halfway moment," says Pearl Buck, "a split second when it can be recalled and perhaps remedied." We must exercise the power of choice to say NO to our own self-doubts, our anxieties, our fears. NO is liberating.

You can't be in two places at once; you can't do two things at once well or with any satisfaction, and you can't do things if your heart isn't in them. When you say NO to something, someone else will gladly embrace saying yes. The universe will provide for everyone who makes sincere choices. Try to always keep what Emerson calls "beautiful limits."

Value your freedom and independence. Think for yourself and act accordingly. What you don't do is as important as what you do. Whether you say no to something because it is not something you care about, because it is a conflict of interest, or because you don't really enjoy the people involved, learn to say NO. You will see that saying NO leads to the life you most want to live.

We do not generally suffer from others; we suffer from ourselves.
I have shown you the way to liberation, now you must take it for yourself.

THE BUDDHA

Stand on Your Own Two Feet

Each step upward makes me feel stronger
and fit for the next step.

GANDHI

With the privilege of being an individual, we have the responsibility to shape and form our life through our choices. Be the person you are meant to become. Be a rugged individualist, a nonconformist. The secondhand thoughts and beliefs you inherited from tradition may very well not be the truth as you've come to know it.

You have to take a stand within yourself. Being tough minded, thinking things through for yourself, is the only way to be able to stand in the center of your essence and think challenging thoughts that bring out truth and clarity as you pursue your extraordinary natural talents. In Emerson's essay "Success," he laments, "It is rare to find a man who believes his own thought or who speaks that which he was created to say. As nothing astonishes men so much as common sense and plain dealing, so nothing is more rare in any man than an act of his own ... Feel yourself, and be not daunted by things ... The light by which we see in this world comes out from the soul of the observer."

Who are some of your heroes throughout history? Who do you look to for inspiration and guidance? Who are some of the brilliant artists who have pointed the way toward transcendent beauty and divine thoughts of unity and love? What poets do you read and study? Who are the spiritual teachers who point the way for you? Who are your favorite presidents? Take a few moments to write down a few of your favorite people, your light bearers, those who have helped you to become a more critical thinker. As a fun exercise, write a few words, a sentence or two, next to the name of someone you greatly admire. For Aristotle, I write, "The good life is the life of excellence, based on the principle of the Golden Triangle of what is true, good, and beautiful, the Golden Mean between the two extremes of too much and too little. Happiness is the aim, the goal, and the purpose of life."

Some of the people I most admire are original thinkers who have struggled to find the truth and wisdom from within their own essential nature, who have been guided by their intuition to be true to their higher self. Michelangelo taught us, "To confide in one's self, and become something of worth and value, is the best and safest course."

Who are you in your core? What do you really think and feel? What do you accept as truth and what do you reject? I was so fortunate to be saved from developing a closed mind when I was taken around the world at sixteen and exposed to radically different cultures. My brilliant aunt was my guide; she saved me by taking me away from a preppy town in Connecticut and thrusting me into the dusty streets of Calcutta. Who I was on the Pan American flight going to Rome and who I was three months later, flying back from Hawaii, were two different people. I grew up fast. I immediately outgrew the petty prejudices, the shallow gossip, and the snickering. Westport, Connecticut, was no longer my whole world. I returned to my studies in New York and never went back to Westport.

This life-changing experience continues to grow in my consciousness each day and has for more than forty-five years. I feel I've been able to accept personal responsibility for my life. I don't blame others or outer circumstances for my unrealized dreams or my unrealistic expectations. I know I'm accountable for the choices I freely make in the training of my own mind through study and contemplation.

Many of us have been brainwashed while growing up. I often say that our task is to unlearn so much of what we've been taught. As we stretch ourselves into the originality of a new idea, we won't lose our sense of gravity. We'll actually feel more security, more grounding in the truth. In Emerson's well-known essay "Self-Reliance," he tells us, "Nothing is at last sacred but the integrity of your own mind. Absolve you to yourself."

In the late 1980s, Peter and I spent many long weekends one summer in Bermuda, where we enjoyed our days writing. During these memorably fun "writer's workshops," I remember teasing Peter as we heard the local church clock bong twelve times, and he hadn't begun to write. "Researching, eh, Peter?" The weekends required writing, arising out of reading, as there comes a time when you have to put pen to paper. It is far easier to read great literature when you don't yet feel ready to plunge into a blank sheet of paper and express something fresh and new.

One of my favorite sayings of the ancient Chinese sage Lao Tzu is "The journey of a thousand miles begins with one step." Challenge yourself to mentally step outside of your family and community, get away from the superficial chitchat in your head and go into the depths of your being to discover who you are, why you are here, what choices you should make to be able to put your innate talents to the best use. The author of *The Little Prince*, Antoine de Saint-Exupéry, taught us, "What saves a man is to take a step. Then another step." On and on and on, we must try with each step we take to listen to our own voice, really believe what we believe, live our own philosophy, and be true to who we are meant to become.

We are pure potential. Striving is our birthright. We're here to grow, to discover, to explore and develop our full powers. When we move onward and upward we're more in control, we push our limits. The higher we climb, the more alive we feel, the happier we are, the more confident we become that our life has meaning. When we choose to stand on our own two feet, we maintain our balance; if we fall, we stand up again. The tougher the challenge, the greater the sense of victory.

My favorite French sixteenth-century essayist Montaigne wrote in *Late Bloomers*, "There is no use our mounting on stilts, for on stilts we must still walk on our own legs." There are great inner resources in each of us.

Stand tall where you are. All the people who accept their responsibility to use their minds and gifts responsibly are adding their originality and inborn talents to the universe.

It is our turn now to carry on this enterprise, making our unique contribution to the world. Any form of imitation is dishonest. We have all the giants from the past to learn from, and then we have to let go and rely on ourselves. There is a Japanese proverb: "Fall seven times, stand up eight." There is greatness inside you. Keep on keeping on, as you choose to use this gift of potential for your own satisfaction and for the benefit of the world. Keep challenging your physical, intellectual, and spiritual choices. Stand up for yourself, stand on your own two feet, and stand tall, firm in your convictions to live up to your higher self.

Rely upon yourself.

THE BUDDHA

Information Is Not Inspiration

Inspiration may be a form of superconsciousness, or perhaps subconsciousness—the antithesis of self-consciousness.

AARON COPLAND

Being inspired is far more enlightening than being informed. I know a great many bright, knowledgable people who are cynical, unhappy, and negative. Many well-informed people are spiritually bankrupt, hollow inside. There is so much more to life than the sum total of facts.

One hundred years ago no one could imagine the flood of information that would be available today. You can drown in it if you're not careful. The Information Age first dawned in the 1970s. An abundant amount of publications were available, along with manipulation of information. Through the use of computers and the Internet, we can now learn about anything we choose to know. We can collect facts and data in an endless stream. The Internet is limitless; it is overwhelming.

The ancient Chinese sage Lao Tzu wrote a thought that rings true in our age of information overload: "Empty and be full." It reminds me of the story of a Zen master who was sharing the tea ceremony with a pupil: the teacher deliberately poured tea into his student's cup until it spilled over onto the table, the floor, and the student's robe. When the student inquired why his master had deliberately poured the hot tea over everything, there was a deep pause, and then the Zen master said, "When your mind is so full of preconceived notions, you have no room for insights and fresh inspiration."

Bob O'Brien, a prize-winning journalist and writer, advised me when

I first began to write not to read the newspaper before I did my work. The human mind has limits to how much it can absorb. We can know everything, yet not know anything about how to live. We have to be careful not to clog our minds with bad news that cannot inspire.

Inner illumination is divine spark. My book designer for many years, a most talented and angelic friend, Marysarah Quinn, would meet with me regularly to have creative sessions. When she worked, she smiled. Once she said with a chuckle, "I don't know what I'd do without divine inspiration." This awareness is not from facts or thoughts, but from a high level of stimulation and inner guidance. In her book *Transformations— Awakening to the Sacred in Ourselves,* Tracy Cochran expresses this beautifully: "Our work feels effortless and we may feel buoyed up by an energy that shows why *inspiration* literally means *infused with spirit or with breath* of the divine. We may feel in sync with the world around us."

What are some of the conditions that stimulate your mind to high, intense feelings? Perhaps a favorite hymn sung by a good choir, or an Impressionism exhibition at a museum, or a magnificent sunset over water. What moves you when you are full of enlivened, exalting emotions? Last summer, when our grandchildren came to our cottage for a visit, we bought some colorful plastic buckets and shovels and some sky-blue watering cans to play with at the beach. Late one afternoon, after returning from several hours at the beach, we all decided to water the blue hydrangea bushes that were in full bloom. They never looked more abundant and breathtakingly beautiful as they surrounded our tiny round patio set with blue-and-white cushioned chairs under a bright blue umbrella. Who could have known that three wee blue watering cans could have aroused such glee in three small children? We giggled as the grandchildren insisted they could almost see the hydrangea grow.

To breathe in this perfect summer afternoon scene in the fresh sea air, to experience this simple tender event, was inspiring. Everything happened spontaneously. We were empty and therefore full. The French existential writer, Albert Camus, understood: "An intense feeling carries with it its own universe."

I study philosophy every day because I know information is not inspiration. I'm trying to absorb and discover as much as I can that is enlightening and inspiring. Rather than filling myself up only with current events, I balance what I read with ancient philosophy in hopes of becoming influenced by its wisdom and vision. I know I will never know very much compared to how much there is to know, but I treasure how I feel about the quality of my life and the integrity of my soul. This is, to me, the main focus of my learning: to try to raise my consciousness to higher and deeper levels of awareness of the beauty of life and all the mysteries that are beyond our knowing.

Professor Emeritus Pierre Hodot of the Collége de France in Paris in his scholarly book *What is Ancient Philosophy?* helps us to understand why we want to gain knowledge: "The point was thus not so much to question the apparent knowledge we think we have, as to question *ourselves* and the values which guide our own lives." Professor Hodot hits the mark when he writes: "The real problem is therefore not the problem of knowing this or that, but of *being* in this way or that."

The important truth to remember is that how we live, how we feel, and how deeply we breathe in the divine spark, defines who we really are. Perhaps we can try to unlearn some of the facts that are no longer true for us. Maybe we should pay close attention to the muse of our poetic instincts. I'd rather breathe in inspiration than be logical or literal. It's a good feeling to know we don't know—and we never will know—the great mysteries.

Life to me is a miracle. Through inspiration we live miracles every day—three sweet grandchildren, three wee sky-blue plastic watering cans, and some thirsty blue hydrangea bushes. When we're receptive, it doesn't take much to feel the breath of the divine.

Inspiration and vision was then, and now is, and I hope will always be, my element, my eternal dwelling place.

WILLIAM BLAKE

We are weaving character every day, and the way to weave the
best character is to be kind and to be useful. Think right, act right;
it is what we think and do that makes us what we are.

ELBERT HUBBARD

There is a natural rebound of contentment and a sense of accomplishment when you choose to do what's right in each situation. Your
choice is between you and you. The right thing may not be convenient
or easy, but when we face the truth, and act, we are building strength of
character. Take whatever pains necessary to do what ought to be done
because this is the way to live a good, decent, honorable life. With free will,
we must be responsible for our clean conscience. Aristotle spoke of this so
beautifully 2,500 years ago when he taught "active virtue": "Happiness
does not consist in pastimes and amusements but in virtuous activities."
When we accept the challenge to do the morally correct thing, to show
compassion and to stay the course, we are rewarded just by having done
the right thing. Plato asked an old man who'd told him he was attending
classes on virtue, "When will you finally begin to live virtuously?" This is
a good question we should all ask ourselves. I love what Abraham Lincoln
once said :"When I do good, I feel good. When I do bad, I feel bad. That
is my religion."

So often I think back to the time my mother was battling cancer. I
remember going on a trip with my family to Italy, which we'd planned a

year in advance, soon after she was diagnosed. I called her every day and realized that when we returned, I'd be the family member who would be her primary caregiver. For ten and a half months I regularly traveled from New York City to a hospital in Connecticut or her home, but mostly to the hospital. I wasn't able to do a good job with my interior design business. I wasn't home to supervise my young daughters or stepson. I wasn't "there" for my husband 100 percent. I was determined to see that my mother received the best care possible and that we spent quality time together right to the end. It wasn't easy. It wasn't fun. But she and I grew to be close; I grew by leaps and bounds in understanding about my mother's difficult life, how meaningful it was to her for us to be together. My commitment to do the best I could for her at the sad end of her life remains deeply satisfying. I feel no guilt about what more I could have done. I gave my all to this tough choice and feel grateful I was there for her.

When thinking through their choices, most people have an innate sense of the right thing to do, of virtue in action. We feel it viscerally. When we act on our choices, we feel more deserving of all the good that pours into us. I know some people have been conditioned to feel unworthy and to "gather up the crumbs." I believe we are all worthy, but life's rewards have to be earned. With such rewards comes a deep sense of integrity. We feel humble, blessed, and glad we chose rightly and did such a good job. We feel stronger, more self-reliant, and more dignified when we bravely face what we must do. We should take great satisfaction in doing the right things for our family and friends. But a most important thing to keep in mind is to be sure we make wise and wonderful choices for ourselves.

Every day we have a fresh opportunity to make good choices that will reward us in the act of doing what is appropriate. Try to always make the true choice in big and little areas of your life. Sacrificing and saving for your children's college education is something most of us naturally choose to do. Declaring every purchase meticulously when you clear customs at an airport, or giving someone full credit when they help you, are choices of character. We should choose to never bend the truth. The choices we make through rigorous discipline expand us, elevate us, and confirm all the good that is our essence. Choose the high right choices, the ones that appear to be best for your life as a whole, and good for everyone else. When we follow the right to the end, we'll always feel satisfied and we'll be in good company.

> I will follow the right even to the fire—
> but avoiding the fire if possible.
>
> **MONTAIGNE**

Go After What You Love

We love everything according to our own goodness.

MEISTER ECKHART

I love the expression "Go for it." We can't expect to find what we love without reaching out for new, exciting experiences. We have approximately 60,000 thoughts a day. That's the good news. The sad news is that 95 percent of the time, we think the same old thoughts. We'll live in a narrow frame of reference unless we choose to search, seek, and find new things to love. The ancient Greek philosopher Sophocles taught us, "Look and you will find it—what is unsought will go undetected." We can expose ourselves to an infinitely vast range of possibilities. We should never wait for good things to come to us. We can go exploring and we'll always find a great number of things to be excited about.

What are some of the ways you uncover and discover new interests, passions, and even obsessions? What are some of the things you love? How did you discover them? Emerson believed that when we have arrived at the question, the answer is already near. Question everything and you will discover what you are looking for and will deepen your knowledge. You might discover that you love roses and want to grow your own. If no one ever promised you a rose garden, you can choose to go after what you love. Where do you begin? You can read up on roses. You can visit different gardens and see what you most adore—what colors, what scents, what varieties thrive best in your climate and soil. By asking gardeners questions and listening carefully to their responses, and by careful observation, you will be able to go to a nursery, buy some rose bushes, and properly plant them. You're not going to be able to wake up on a beautiful summer morning, with the dew still on the ground, and run out barefoot and see the splendid beauty of your rose garden unless you choose to make it happen.

I've discovered that once we're excited about something—anything—we'll naturally be attracted to helpful people who are experts or professionals or avid amateurs who love to share their knowledge. Through our mutual interest in art or music or bird watching or tennis, we find great stimulation in our time spent together.

Your passions can lead to professional enrichment as well. Thomas Edison had an ingenious perception about light. He passionately pursued his interest, experimenting—being wrong 99 percent of the time. But he was able to invent the light bulb and forever changed the way we live our lives. Sometimes we unveil what we love by admitting what we don't love. I admit I do not love opera. I've been exposed to opera all of my life, beginning with my grandmother, who wanted to be an opera singer. I loved her, but I couldn't bear hearing her sing. Opera aside, I came to love many other types of classical music, and I often listen to classical music on the radio when I'm at my desk.

I love the ballet and am inspired when I experience a fine performance. When I go to a concert and hear beautiful music, because I'm so visual, I miss the beauty of the ballerinas: their colorful costumes, the stage set. It isn't as interesting to me to watch a musician play his or her instrument as it is to watch the grace and harmony of great dancers as I hear the magnificent music. Some people would prefer to go to a ball game than to the ballet.

When people tell me they haven't found their passion, I suggest that they read ancient philosophy, which encourages taking pleasure in a variety of different things, choosing the ones that we are the best fit for, and thus identifying certain interests that we want to pursue over other possibilities.

Most of us agree that loving what we're doing, loving what we see, hear, smell, taste, and touch increases our sense of happiness and pleasure. I have a friend who has recently taken up quilting. In the community in Florida where Barbara lives, she met an expert quilter at her book club. She was invited to go to one of her classes. What did she have to lose? Barbara enjoys sewing and loves color and pretty textiles. From the minute she was exposed to the idea of actually creating her own quilts, she was hooked.

A friend sold his boat because his family had so many interests, including a daughter who is a nationally ranked tennis player. Life changed and he wanted to be there for his daughter, to coach her in her tournaments. He discovered that when he was at home, he loved to do woodworking— something not possible on a boat. Garry now makes furniture in the heated garage of his Wisconsin house and gives his elegant pieces to his grandchildren. How did he discover his love of woodworking? Garry believes having the boat for so long, with all its beautiful woodwork, made him appreciate fine woods and excellent workmanship. But had he not sold his boat to pursue other interests, he might not have had the opportunity to discover this new passion.

Whether you pursue golf, tennis, fishing, sailing, painting, cooking, or playing the flute, whatever you choose, you will put in long patient hours of experimenting, perfecting your skills, sharpening your tools, learning as you go. We will continue to find new things we love, and we'll pursue them throughout the course of our lifetimes. Aristotle wisely reminds us, "It is the nature of desire not to be satisfied."

When we choose to live a good life, we will make choices in every area of our existence that will improve our well-being. Robert Louis Stevenson wrote "To know what you prefer ... is to have kept your soul alive." Let us see what we love so we may know our spirits better.

Many intellectual, well-meaning people have not kept their souls alive because they have been afraid to express themselves honestly. We are all creative because we are creating our lives, choice by choice. We have to have an intimate connection with the choices we make about people, places, and things. There is no area of our lives that we cannot make richer or fuller. We've barely tapped the surface of our human potential.

Try different things until something clicks. One thing will definitely lead to another. There's no such thing as a person with too many interests. We become interesting when we're engaged in things we love. The good, big, fun life is waiting for us. Take pleasure in discovering what truly excites you, and then go after all your stimulating discoveries. Watch the universe come toward you as though you're a magnet of good energy.

The supreme good—to examine everything—a life which was not devoted to such research would not be worth living. Happiness would thus consist in their never-ending quest.

PLATO

8

Have Realistic Expectations

To take what there is, and use it, without waiting forever in vain for the preconceived—to dig deep into the actual and get something out of that—this doubtless is the right way to live.

HENRY JAMES

The wisest way to live is to choose to enjoy what is actually available to you right now, right here. We learn to see the world of abundance, not limits, through training our minds. Whenever we become attached to the outcome, an end result, that we have preconceived, we deprive ourselves of experiencing joy. Choose not to be sad about what you don't have but to be glad with what you have.

So many interior design clients were utterly unreasonable in expecting and even demanding their job to be completed by an unrealistic date. I had a client once who threatened that if the handcrafted Canadian maple four-poster bed was not in place in her island home's master bedroom by Labor Day, she would not pay for it. This demand allowed seven days to somehow complete the cabinetwork and hire a shipper to get it to the house by boat. I had custom-designed this bed; it had removable ball finials to allow easily changing a variety of bed-hangings, and chamfered bedposts that were gracefully beveled to soften the corners. An artistic cabinetmaker was soulfully, meticulously, creating the bed. I knew his wife was ill with cancer; I chose not to mention this outlandish demand to him. I simply told the client I wasn't able to meet her deadline and I had the bed delivered to me in mid-autumn and paid for it myself. Peter and I are the happy ones who have had the blessing of sleeping in this handsome bed all these years.

When we accept reality—not fixating on how we wish things to be—we will be less disappointed in ourselves, in others, and in life in general. It's a good choice to regularly give ourselves a reality check to determine if our circumstances or expectations conform to the truth. When we gladly face the true, the real, the actual, we're able to let go of the myth, the dream, and the unrealistic. Why should we expect more than is literally possible? None of us embraces failure, but we often set ourselves up for disappointment when we ask or expect more than is realistic.

The champion tennis player Martina Navratilova understood that "the moment of victory is much too short to live for that and nothing else." Few of us ever achieve complete victory, but we can all live good and successful lives. When Andy Roddick lost to Roger Federer in three straight sets in the Men's Finals at Wimbledon in 2005, he was realistic: "It is difficult to kick oneself when the goal seems so far out of reach." Federer, whose grass-court victory streak was then at thirty-six, understood: "It's hard for him; you know, this is my best match maybe that I've ever played." When we focus on playing the best game we can, win or lose, this is our personal victory.

A recent study showed that Olympic athletes who only focus on being victorious, being number one, winning the gold medal, are depressed when they win the silver or bronze prize. If we are too tough a taskmaster, we are unable to find pleasure in how well we are doing. A well-lived life is not always about winning or losing, but about playing the game, doing our best learning from the process, and accepting that there is grace and dignity in being a good loser. The good life doesn't require us to be number one.

Many respected philosophers believe it is important for us to discover and come to grips with our limitations, with what we cannot do. Who is it that once made the brilliant remark, "You have to choose to sail according to the wind"? We are all capable of an enormous amount of good, but in our brief lifetime, we have limitations—we can't be good at everything, nor are we going to have everything happen just the way we wish. Expected the unexpected. Things will happen. They will catch us off guard unless we are prepared. When we have a contingency plan in place, we don't need to panic when the unknown becomes known.

Many of my readers tell me that they are frightened by the post-9/11, post-Katrina world we live in. All the more reason to be realistic and to plan and choose well. Believe in the life you *are* living. Receive the gift of life as it is, with glad heart. You now know how much worse off you could be. You could be homeless or could have lost family members, or be dead. Everything that happens gives us a fresh opportunity to open our hearts to a wider view.

A scientific textbook *Well-Being: The Hedonics of Pleasure and Pain,* is full of studies illustrating that when people have unrealistic expectations, they set themselves up for unhappiness and depression. This in-depth international study of happiness makes it crystal clear that all of our experiences in life are about opposites and contrast. There is truth and falsehood, old and young, light and dark, sun and shade, health and illness, pleasure and pain, joy and sorrow, war and peace, hot and cold, love and hate, wealth and poverty, desire and fear, ups and downs, beauty and ugliness, happiness and depression, good and bad, life and death.

We only understand happiness because we have felt unhappy. We know inner peace because we have felt turmoil. We feel comfort because we have been uncomfortable. The practical philosopher Benjamin Franklin instructed us, "Take one thing with another, and the world is a pretty good sort of a world, and it is our duty to make the best of it, and be thankful." My daughter Brooke once said, laughing, "Life is so random." There's good and there's bad. This statement is wise because we have to understand the coexistence of opposite values.

Deepak Chopra, a noted pioneer doctor in exploring the mind-body connection, expressed this truth well: "When a person quietly reconciles himself to all the contradictions that life offers, and can comfortably ride out or flow between the banks of pleasure and pain, experiencing them both, but getting stuck in neither, then he has achieved freedom." Understanding the meaning of coexistence of opposite values is key to freedom. Our lives are meaningless unless we accept that literally all experiences in life are understood by contrast. When we know what it feels like to be hungry, we're more appreciative when we feel satisfied after a delicious meal.

Horrible things happen to us that are outside of our power to choose. Our choice then is to make the very best of what is. We are never in a choice-less moment. We can always choose the greatest good in every situation. The author of the famous Serenity Prayer, Reinhold Niebuhr, helps us to keep things in perspective: "Grant me the serenity to accept the things I cannot change, the courage to change the things I can, and the wisdom to know the difference."

Unrealistic expectations cut both ways. One of the saddest aspects of poverty is the pathetic lack of expectations for a good life. The *New York Times* columnist David Brooks wrote, "The poor drop out of high school, so it seemed normal to drop out of high school. Many teenaged girls had babies, so it seemed normal to become a teenaged mother. It was hard for men to get stable jobs, so it was not abnormal for them to commit crimes and hop from one relationship to another." We need to do what we can to raise the expectations and hopes of the poor who have not been exposed to the example of certain standards of excellence of behavior. A realistic attitude frees us to work hard to change the things we can.

Let us train our minds to desire what the situation demands.
It is best to bear what can't be altered.
SENECA

9

Live from the Inside Out

Things may happen *to* you, but the only things that matter
are the things that happen *in* you.

ERIC BUTTERWORTH

How many people do you know who truly don't care what other people think of them? Few, if any, to be sure. How many people, do you believe, dare to be true to themselves?

How we look, how we dress, where we live, how we live, where we went to school, where we work, how we are accepted by society, are all painfully important to a large number of Americans today. Since World War II, we have been economically twice as well off financially, but we are no happier. What has gone wrong? So many Americans felt that if they acquired wealth they would be looked up to, they would be important, and they would be happy.

Perhaps it is time to review a preeminent and provocative best-selling book, *The Lonely Crowd: A Study of the Changing American Character*, written by sociologist David Riesman and published in 1950. This scholarly book unexpectedly tapped a deep vein of self-criticism among Americans, prompting millions to begin characterizing their friends, neighbors, and associates as "other-directed," "inner-directed," and "tradition-directed." Professor Riesman reported that in periods of technological progress and population growth, people tended to develop a capacity to go it alone and set lifelong goals for themselves based on values such as wealth, fame, the search for scientific truth, the quest for religious salvation, and the creation of beauty. People desperately reach for materialism without achieving happiness. He said that in periods when we consumed more than we produced, and the population growth was flat or in decline, society became less dynamic. As a result, people became more "other-directed," seeking to be accepted into the mainstream by conforming to the expectation and behavior of their peers. But, as we know, we can never please everyone. When we try to, we often create a false front, changing ourselves depending on who we're trying to impress.

The sociologist Dennis H. Wrong believed that *The Lonely Crowd*— a book with the primary intention to analyze, not criticize, American life, was interpreted as a book "deploring the rise of the psychological disposition called 'other-directed' at the expense of 'inner-direction.'" Professor Wrong said it came across as "a trumpet call to some sort of remedial action."

I refer to being "other-directed" as "outer-directed." When we're insecure, we desperately want others to understand us. We try hard to conform to what is going on around us. We want to be liked. But when we like ourselves, when we can be true to who we really are, we don't have to prove ourselves to anyone. When we're wise we make the choice to go inside for guidance. When we mature, we become our own judge. We should always try to live according to our own inner compass, to be responsible for our own life. As we become more and more inner-directed, we will not be afraid to be a nonconformist.

In Professor Riesman's book *Individualism Reconsidered and Other Essays,* he wrote, "What is feared as failure in American society is, above all, aloneness. And aloneness is terrifying because it means there is no one, no group, no approved cause, to submit to." I can't imagine how painful it would be if I didn't like being alone. I'm never lonely when I'm alone because I like to be in my own company, to be by myself, with my own thoughts. Until we are no longer lonely when we're alone, we will always feel lonely in a crowd. The only way to live the good life is from the inside out.

The spiritual leader Eric Butterworth preached that we must always be true to who we are in our core. He wrote and taught about "self-worth-ship," and said that we must live from our own center and not in the "whirling circumference of life." Throughout my lifetime, I've somehow managed to observe and be involved in amazing chaos; yet I've always tried to keep my integrity, and not cave in to violating my essence, even under threatening circumstances.

We "close our eyes to see," as Picasso once said. We go inside for truth, for our core principles, for our deepest desires, our highest ideals. We have goals, we have standards, we have a mission, and we internally inculcate these values and character traits into our life. We can take in all of the outside world, absorbing all the good that inspires us, all the beauty that exalts us, all the love that transforms us. But we must close our eyes, go inside, be still, and listen for our voiceless presence in order to remain true to our authentic self.

Consciously choose to make this your priority—to think for yourself. Meditate over this truth. Your self-talk and self-listening, your self-affirming and self-reflecting, transcend anything and everything that is "other-directed" or "outer-directed." Follow your conscience to experience your inner illumination and follow, follow, follow.

> Find the nerve to be oneself when that self is not approved of
> by the dominant ethic of a society.
>
> **DAVID RIESMAN**

Celebrate Simple Ceremonies

Rituals are so lacking in today's society
that we are impoverished for it.

JACK LENOR LARSEN

All we have in life is what is in front of us. The best way to live well is to put a magnifying glass up to the common, making and creating little rituals, ceremonies, and celebrations as we flow through the day. What a joyful way to choose to live our brief life, not taking anything for granted, being aware, being present to all the sensuous delights available to us, right where we are.

How dreadful to go through life with one long "to do" list, working at everything so hard that we're exhausted, anxious, and burned out. There are big once-in-a-lifetime events that shouldn't have to be fraught with tension. We are meant to enjoy our own wedding ceremony, not be glad when it is over. You plan and plan and plan and then the big day is here. Are you here? Are you in a position to feel the great joy of your commitment and love? Are you present, fully concentrating on the meaning of the ritual, the beauty of the ceremony, the music, the flowers, family and loved ones?

Some people find it difficult to truly enjoy their own dinner parties because they are so busy *doing* that they aren't *being* relaxed and receptive to the conversation and enjoyment of being a host, having loved ones in their home.

One of the greatest pleasures in life is to choose to create everyday ceremonies for living well, for our own sense of contentment and happiness.

If we are accustomed to delicious food and attractive surroundings, a dinner gathering among friends is great fun. Take the image of the wedding day. Think how many little details went into the planning. The more enjoyment one feels from the details of the preparation, the greater the feelings of satisfaction when the actual day unfolds. I have two married daughters, so I'm well aware of all the stress that is related to a wedding, regardless of how small and relatively simple you choose the event to be. Wouldn't it be sad, however, if this big day were not fully lived joyfully? And how great it is to make little celebrations out of all the stages of planning.

Brooke was married on her birthday. She fully enjoyed opening presents at breakfast and writing notes to her bridesmaids, losing track of time. Alexandra, Brooke, and I were so late for our long-scheduled beauty treatments that it seemed we arrived only to pay the bill. We had a good laugh.

You have the gift of choosing your attitude about ordinary days. You can surprise yourself with pleasure at every turn. If you hear a favorite wedding march on the classical music station, you and your spouse can hug and embrace in spontaneous recognition of your wedding day, no matter how many years ago it was. When you greet life choice by choice, detail by detail, aware of how much more happiness you can experience when you deliberately make the most of every human experience, you will be living a good life.

No matter how quiet or humble, everything matters. You are nourishing your soul when you elevate your days into sacred experiences. Choose to be open to these opportunities to celebrate small ceremonies. I've made a ritual of summer mornings at the cottage. I make coffee and then go out into our tiny backyard. I walk around among the flowers and plants. I put tablecloths on the tables and cushions on the chairs. Sometimes I water the plants, sometimes I deadhead and prune, and often I cut some blossoms to bring inside to arrange small bouquets. But I always sit quietly with a tiny view of the harbor, sip my freshly brewed coffee, and meditate until Peter comes out to greet me.

The key to feeling the rapture is not to be in a rush. Let your experience spontaneously unfold. Wherever you are, whatever you are experiencing, concentrate completely, become one with the flowers you are arranging, or the table you are setting, or the tea ceremony you are experiencing, or the cross-stitch you are working on. In this mindful awareness, in this receptive trance, you will awaken your senses to a heightened sensitivity and deepened sense of gratitude. Sounds will be more beautiful, colors more vibrant, more intense, smells more appealing, and taste appreciation will be elevated. When we eat more mindfully, for example, we don't need to doctor up our food as much because we are awake to all the receptors that are part of our sensuous inheritance. You find that you like corn on the cob without salt and butter, and organic beefsteak tomatoes are sublime with a lemon twist and lime juice.

Be silent as you move about in this self-induced state of bliss. Deliberately choose to make a tiny ritual of washing your hands with a special bar of yellow, lemon-scented soap sent to you as a gift from a friend. The carved flower design is pretty and you smell the freshness of the lemon. The hand towel—a heavenly blue tone that reminds you of the sky on a sunny August afternoon—looks so pretty next to the yellow of the soap, reminding you of the sun and sky.

The next time you cut open a cantaloupe, honeydew, or watermelon for breakfast, get out the melon scoop and make balls of the ripe melon. I love to make melon balls because I enjoy eating my food with colorful chopsticks. Eating with chopsticks enhances my celebration of eating delicious healthy food. When you set the table, use your best wedding china to remind you whom it is for, as well as why you have pretty things. Having friends over should be as natural and easy as pulling up some extra chairs. What you do when you're alone should be as beautiful as when you have family and friends over. Sometimes when we have large celebrations, we don't have enough of our finest china, crystal, and silver to go around, so intimate gatherings can be the most refined and special.

When we love ourselves, when we love our home and take great pleasure in it, when we are alone, it is obvious we will feel great pride in sharing our private world with others. Do you have a pitcher of yellow roses on the kitchen table in a favorite hand-painted pitcher? Do you use an underplate to add elegance to the appearance of a cup of soup or a salad? Do you use colorful napkins for everyday meals? Create little rituals that awaken a greater intensity, a more vital love of life. I find that the more little moments I appreciate alone, the greater my ability to embrace and enjoy the company of others. When we celebrate our inner resources privately, we are in a position to share them with others more authentically.

Some people have a specific place and time for their meditation. I believe we should consider meditation not so much a method for stress management but a pathway toward greater inner light. When we ritualize our life, we expose goodness and hidden beauty everywhere. In this consciousness, we can meditate whenever and wherever we are.

Last summer Peter and I were having lunch at a nearby restaurant on a dock overlooking the Stonington harbor. It was one of those magical moments when a refreshing breeze was blowing after days of blistering heat. A cup of cold gazpacho appeared, served by a friend, Ainslie, who runs the restaurant. "I made this from all the fresh vegetables from the farmers' market—tomatoes, cucumbers, cilantro, onions, peppers, and herbs. I thought it would be refreshing for you before you enjoy your lobster salad." She served this ambrosia in stemmed glasses on cobalt-blue plates, garnished with fresh green and purple basil from her own garden. We were surprised and delighted, and we've never had better gazpacho in our lives than Ainslie's.

One of our small ceremonies when we go to Ainslie's restaurant is that we "BYO" organic tomatoes, grown in nearby Rhode Island by Max, whose tomatoes are the best I've ever tasted. We bring our own blue-and-white-handled tomato knife that has a sharp serrated edge. Often Ainslie wants to plate our tomato in the kitchen. This magical day, she chose to go wild! Out came a large blue glass plate brimming with organic greens, buffalo mozzarella cheese balls, big slices of the tomato with chopped basil, Italian parsley, and the best olive oil that looked bright chartreuse on the cheese. Sometimes when you're extremely lucky, when you have good friends, when the weather is perfect, you can have a surprise pleasure that turns into a grand celebration for two.

When corn is in season, treat your family to Sunday night supper of corn on the cob, some ripe tomatoes, and some watermelon. When my daughters were young, one night a week we'd order in Chinese food. I'd put the foods in lacquered bowls and we'd eat with chopsticks. There's no need to cook Chinese food if we can order it on the telephone and have it delivered to our door. In the winter months, Sunday night was soufflé night. We made the soufflés together.

Whether you have a festive picnic at the beach or have a ritual of all holding hands at the dinner table before you begin your meal, your pleasure will bring lasting happiness if you continue to create these little happy moments for yourself and others that give life more meaning.

Start your own list of ways to appreciate the little pleasures around you. Choose to celebrate small ceremonies, capturing the moments tenderly. Let these small acts interconnect all you think and do, making you more fully aware of ways you can live a good life every day.

* Enjoy the scent of roses in your clothes because you hung them on the clothesline near your rose bushes.

* Have a cool shower on a hot, steamy afternoon.

* Clean out your wallet.

* Take a nap in a hammock.

* Walk your dog on a beach.

* Discover a new recipe and try it out on your spouse.

* Enjoy a young wine from a far-off vineyard to celebrate an anniversary.

* Take a back road you've never been on before, even if it is a detour.

- When you travel, put personal things around your hotel room.

- Go on an appreciation walk to peek into all your neighbors' gardens.

- After dinner, go outside and sit and watch the stars and moon.

- Go to a pretty spot, sit in a comfortable chair, and begin to read a new book by a favorite author.

- Sit at your desk, select a beautiful card or postcard and stamp, and write a love letter to a child.

- The next time there is a sudden rain, put on some rubber garden shoes and go look for a rainbow.

- Water the grass in your bare feet. Go under the sprinkler and watch the prisms of light in the droplets.

- Sit down with a cup of tea and slowly read a sweet letter from a dear friend.

- Sing to the birds as you put food in their feeder.

- Unpack groceries mindfully, enjoying the ritual of placement.

- When paying bills, writing cards, or working at your desk, be alert to the whiteness and smoothness of paper, the color and scent of ink, the color of your pencils and erasers.

- Make an attractive ritual of changing the bed linens. Spray some favorite scent on the clean sheets.

- Iron a napkin or a blouse.

- Wrap a pretty package for a gift you're giving.

- Send an article to a friend.

- Water the plants.

- Draw a bath for your love.

- Give a backrub to your spouse.

- Sit looking at a favorite view and thoughtfully contemplate how blessed you are.

* Make iced tea with lemon and lime and mint from the garden or windowsill pot.

* Lay out your clothes before you dress.

* Rearrange the objects on your desk.

* After you have a haircut, go to Starbucks and treat yourself to some time alone and enjoy an iced latté.

Many pleasures cost next to nothing. Surprise yourself with pleasure in the little things in your life. There's joy in these surprises. Choose to thrust yourself into these experiences with devotion and love. Be alert to the richness of how you feel. Be attentive. Pay attention. All the details that go into a rich, full, good life are right here, right now. When you forget this truth and you get caught up in a frenzy, rushing around, stop, flop down on the bed or a sofa or a chair, and breathe deeply for ten counts—vow not to rob yourself of these wondrous joys. Then get going, get back in gear, but with a clear head and more sensitive spirit. Make the big choice to celebrate simple ceremonies. This is the good life, right here, now.

The purpose of life is to express love in all its manifestations.

TOLSTOY

11

Reevaluate Your Priorities Regularly

The mind has no pre-existing ideas or concepts. The mind creates its own agenda out of what happens to it.

JACQUES BARZUN

We're free to choose the best, most important things to do, depending on the circumstances. Consistency in our choosing is not to be praised: don't be proud that you are consistent. The only great certainty is uncertainty. We're given this great gift of choice so we can choose wisely in changing times. It is precisely through the tough choices we're willing to make that we're able to carve out a life of excellence where real good is achieved.

We fine-tune our lives choice by choice, much the same way a harpist plucks at the strings of the harp to create beautiful music. She has to select the right strings, at the right time, to create grace in the sound. In our life, we have to choose the right strings to pluck. We do this by reevaluating what is currently important. Life is like an ever-flowing river. Events and circumstances are in flux; they come and go. We undergo internal as well as external changes continuously bubbling up and affecting our priorities. How we feel at the time will guide our choices.

We should be flexible in our priorities. Have Plan B in place when Plan A isn't appropriate. Because of the rain, the planned picnic at the beach is now going to become a trip to the aquarium, lunch at home, and a visit to the library. Rigidly planning events you can't control only leads to frustration and disappointment. Your life shouldn't be fixed by long-range plans that can trip you up and cause you problems when circumstances change. Let the future unfold naturally.

I knew a conscientious woman who married an older man. She spent her days and nights worrying and planning for *his* old age. She even bought a condominium on the beach in Naples, Florida, for his retirement years. Surprise. She died young of cancer and he remarried, never retired, and died at ninety-two, having played eighteen holes of golf that day. You just never know. Who is absolutely certain about anything?

We should question our priorities regularly, asking ourselves what really makes sense now. The past can shed some light on our direction, but the path we're on may be entirely different from the one that was appropriate for us five or ten years ago. When we're honest with ourselves, we may find that many of us were brainwashed into certain belief systems that are no longer true for us. In order to have strong personal convictions, we have to be brave enough to change our life around. We do this by reevaluating our priorities.

Many of the cells in our body are new after a few days or several years. What always was may no longer be our tradition or belief. We always had the family to our home for the holidays, for example. Now we go—when we're invited—to be with the grandchildren. "Santa Claus doesn't come down Big Mommy's chimney." We have to share these holidays with other grandparents and family because of our daughter's marriage, as well as my divorce. Choices aren't always sweet, but they are empowering when we adapt well to what is happening.

I remember years ago being in a state of shock when Peter was having emergency knee surgery. I called my daughter Alexandra and said he must recover quickly and go to rehabilitation because I had a busy lecture schedule on the West Coast. Alexandra immediately realized I wasn't thinking clearly and gently told me there was no way I could leave Peter. I ended up canceling six lectures from a pay phone in the hospital lobby while he was being operated on.

If someone you love has a health crisis, you quickly readjust your priorities. One of the great principles in decorating that my mentor Eleanor Brown taught her designers is that when one thing changes in a room, you have to rethink everything. This rule of Mrs. Brown's applies to all aspects of life. There is a chain reaction among all things because of their interconnection. We should certainly set up our lives in a pleasant manner, thinking and planning ahead, but being open and receptive to what is real *now*. Be willing to give up old patterns, old familiar ways of being, in order to open up to a new way of seeing your life, with fresh beginnings that bring great meaning.

Feel free to question your core values and what you most love, what you feel are the best choices for you, as circumstances radically change for better or for worse. The author Robert Louis Stevenson expressed it well: "To change one's mind in changing circumstances is true wisdom."

Years ago I received a windfall that took me completely by surprise. There was an auction for publication rights to my book *Living a Beautiful Life*. A check eventually came in the mail from my literary agent's office. "Wow!" This was an "aha" moment. It was so unexpected, so magical, so wonderful, I sat down with Peter and said, "Let's go to France and Italy. Let's stay a month. Let's come back empty handed." And that's just what we did. We reevaluated our priorities by splurging on an expensive trip we never would or could have taken without this windfall. This was a once-in-a-lifetime gift. We used it to live a beautiful life together in Provence and Tuscany, places we love that had brought us great happiness in the past; places with authentic character and charm that always enchant us. When some sudden good comes our way, we should take advantage of the opportunity it offers.

Every choice you make is going to have a ripple effect of consequences. If you choose to marry or if you decide to have children, these serious decisions will require continuous reevaluating of your priorities because of all the unknown circumstances they bring. Perhaps you earn a promotion or are out of work or you relocate to another part of the country because of a job offer. Wouldn't it be wonderful if we could choose to live in a desired place, move there, and then find a job we would enjoy? When we reevaluate our priorities regularly, we might consider relocating. Maybe there is a more suitable place to live that matches our temperament. Or perhaps we don't want the maintenance of the large house now that the children have their own homes and families.

Our lives will always be in transition. Are your wise choices of yesterday relevant today? The charities you gave money to may shift as you gain fresh knowledge of other needs and concerns that interest you. Who you invite to a party changes as your friends do. Who you give gifts to may vary over the years. People move away, they fade away, and they die. Your financial situation changes. You've taken up new interests. You decide you want to travel more.

Be comfortable with your restless nature. Choose not to be settled. Last summer a good friend who was spending his summer in Ireland asked me what Peter and I were doing for the summer. I smiled at Walter and said, "I don't know." What a liberating feeling not to know what I was doing. I was simply aware I was going to be at the cottage most of the summer. I had no set plans. As a consequence, it was the happiest summer of my adult life because I gave myself the gift of time.

If your business is slow, you can make the good choice to take up painting watercolors, or to spend more time playing tennis. If your child requires a series of medical procedures, you can choose to take out a bank loan in order to be assured he has the best possible care. If your elderly father is terminally ill, you can arrange for him to live with you or at a nearby hospice. If you discover after a semester of college you chose to attend that you are unhappy because the isolated environment of the campus doesn't suit you, you can apply to another college in a city.

If you are divorced or your husband dies and your children are all grown, you may decide to move to a new state and live in a small cottage near a beach, or you may want to move nearer to where your children live. Peter became a nonpracticing lawyer a few years ago in order to be my full-time partner and be more free to travel with me. He often said that his practice of law for fifty-six years was the most stimulating and rewarding experience of his life. But it was time to close that chapter and move on.

We live our lives in chapters. When we get older, we may want to live in a village where we can walk about rather than be isolated in rural country. Perhaps you've spent most of your marriage primarily caring for your children when your husband was busy with international business travel. Now the children are adults with their own families, your husband is retired, and you're free to care for him. The good life requires adaptation.

If you've been caring for a sick child who is now healing well, you're free now to make it your priority to spend more time taking care of yourself. You can now practice yoga, do more meditation, and give yourself more time to read good books that help your soul to grow. If you've had to work hard for years to earn money to raise your children and save for their college expenses, you're now able to choose to spend time traveling with your spouse. You may no longer want the big city apartment, but would prefer a simpler, more carefree life together in the country in the peace and beauty of nature with easy access to golf, tennis, and sailing. I once spent 75 to 85 percent of my time running an interior design business. Now I spend the equivalent of that amount of time writing and traveling to give lectures.

All of life is paradoxical. Be ready, at any moment, to make fresh, bold choices that will enable you to make the most good of whatever happens. Things will always be different. We replace one thing with another. Flow with the currents of the river of life, living peacefully and happily with growth and change as you deepen your sense of satisfaction and appreciation of all our privileges.

We must be willing to get rid of the life we've planned,
so as to have the life that is waiting for us.

JOSEPH CAMPBELL

Have as Few Regrets as Possible

For of all sad words of tongue or pen, the saddest are these:
It might have been!

JOHN GREENLEAF WHITTIER

Sometimes the truth hits us over the head and we literally realize we *are* our choices. We own the good ones, the bad ones, the ones that cause us a great deal of pain, as well as the ones that give us our greatest pleasures. If we always make wise, wonderful choices, we will be able to live with no regrets.

All of us identify with our mistakes, our failures of judgment, and the choices that were wrong for us for whatever reasons. When we are honest with ourselves, we're able to admit our mistakes, what we could have done that we didn't do, or what we did do that was not wise or appropriate. You marry the wrong person, you take shortcuts on the job, you stay too long in a teaching job when you really wanted to try your hand at being an artist. Or maybe you didn't show up for a really important life event for a child and you can't make this wrong choice go away.

We suffer huge pain for some of the choices we've made that were harmful to others or to us. When we find ourselves in these difficult situations, we have to live with the consequences of our bad choices. Free will requires us to make choices and then live with them. We pay the price for whatever we do and don't do. With freedom comes responsibility and accountability, but not being free to make our own choices is simply not an option.

One of the most difficult situations arises when we become involved with others we later discover have problems—all kinds of problems. How can we be true to ourselves, to our values and boundaries, when other people in our life act badly? Rationally, we understand that we can't get swept up in everyone else's problems and, yet, realistically, we are involved. What if your single daughter becomes pregnant or your boss goes to jail or your sister has an affair, your child marries a bad person, your husband is disloyal to you, or someone blackmails you? What if your mother is an alcoholic? How can we stay true to ourselves when chaos reigns? How can we remain trustworthy when there are people in our close circle who frankly are off their path? How can we keep our dignity intact? How can we choose to be empathetic, loving, and compassionate without being dragged down by the others' situations? How can we be helpful without harming our emotional balance? How can we choose to do the right thing when others we trusted let us down?

What about the times when we were in denial or didn't listen to others or to our own inner voice? I love the words of Nikos Kazantzakis, whose beloved character Zorba in *Zorba the Greek* urged him to pay attention, to hear: "If I had listened to his voice—not his voice, his cry—my life would have acquired value." Kazantzakis is talking about his fictional character Zorba, who Kazantzakis most wanted to emulate. We all make many mistakes. But we also can admit them and learn wisdom from them, and be guided in the future toward greater understanding and better choices. Example can be everything if we hear the cry and act, but most of us don't. We usually have to learn the hard, painful way.

We never fail when we admit our error, move on, grow through it, and come out of it a better, happier person. I have a good friend who is a "successful" lawyer. She makes a lot of money but is working with a bunch of aggressive men who don't respect women, who are fiercely driven, and who try to drive her crazy. They have no boundaries. She has to choose to change professions, or at least law firms, if she is going to find happiness.

What are some of your deep regrets? Do you wish you had taken that last family trip together when everyone was still healthy, now that your parents are both dead? Do you regret that you didn't go back and finish graduate school after your child went to college? Do you regret choosing the wrong life partner, feeling stuck in a dreadful marriage, and being too numb to leave? Do you regret taking on a business partner who turned out to be dishonest? Are you sorry for angry outbursts when you said things you deeply regret? Have you ever been mean or rude? Have you ever been put in a compromising situation when you lowered your own standard of excellence because others weren't doing their share, when you chose to coast because you thought, "Why bother?"

What are you making of yourself when those around you are lazy and indifferent? What are you doing with your life? It's never too late to choose to change yourself. Do not give up or run away from the opportunity to grow. That is the ultimate tragedy. There's no place to go and hide in life. Your job, your duty, your responsibility, is to make the most you can of you. If everyone chose to do this, the world would be a peaceful, happy paradise. Don't regret that you were unable to shape up others; only regret when you don't live up to your own vast potential for good.

Work on yourself *every* day. We can't sprint at the end and catch up. We need to strengthen our intellectual muscles now before our brain loses synapses. We need to build upon our virtuous habits of choice every single day in order to have fewer and fewer regrets.

Don't be afraid to do what only you can do. Rather than having chest pains trying to do work you no longer are capable of or enjoy, it may be better to cut your losses. You will feel great joy and satisfaction doing something you know you love to do. What would you choose to do if you knew you couldn't fail? Do that very thing, because it is there where you'll develop your potential. You and I are capable of so much more. We should encourage each other to do more to express who we are. We can cut through our difficulties by our belief in our self. The only way we can fail is not to try. Michelangelo wrote: "The greatest danger for most of us is not that our aim is too high and we miss it, but that it is too low and we reach it."

Our consciousness is ours to raise as high as we're able, as soon as possible. We all have lots of work to do. All of our experiences give us knowledge and inspiration to build on. Our glass, we will discover, is more than half full. Fill it up. Let it brim over. Use all your powers while you can. It is tragedy to die before we're fully born. We can't afford to let our creative spirit die inside while we're still able to make life-changing choices. We're only using a fraction of our capacity. All the rush and frantic busy-ness is keeping us from the good choices that will allow us to live with as few regrets as possible.

One choice I persistently try to make is to be persevering. When we stay the course, when we keep trying, we will have fewer regrets. Perseverance leads to good habits that help us over the inevitable rough patches. Live with an appreciative awareness of the precious gift of your life. Don't miss the mark by not making your own brave choices. This is your challenge. Don't feel sorry for what might have been. You are your choices. Own your choices. Hear the cry and choose to follow what is the good life for you.

Forgive me for saying so, boss, but you're just a pen-pusher. Here you had the chance of a lifetime to see a beautiful green stone, and you didn't see it.

NIKOS KAZANTZAKIS,

ZORBA THE GREEK

Leave the Safe Harbor

There is only one true heroism, and that is to know the
world as it is and to love it. The great people of history, certainly
the spiritually great, give evidence of this ability.

HUGH DOWNS

Who do you look up to? Who are your heroes? Who do you know who has great courage and strength, who dares to do what is noble and adventurous? Whose bold exploits inspire you to live more vitally, to dare more beautifully?

Many people whine about all their problems, complaining that their ship hasn't come in. What they don't recognize is that they've never left the dry dock. When you stay safe and sound at shore, you'll never set sail and really choose the good life. How sad to realize that many people die within five miles of where they were born, having been afraid to explore the unknown. My father, for example, often said with a chuckle, "You can't trust the French." But how did he know? He never went to France.

You have to start somewhere. Choose a harbor near you and explore the exciting opportunities and challenges awaiting you. Whether you go on a ride in a car, a boat, a train, or a plane, or you choose to go hiking or on horseback, don't stay where it's comfortable and safe. Get moving. Get going. Let the exciting adventure begin.

When you compare how relatively easy it is for us to travel today, compared to one hundred years ago, we have no excuse not to choose to explore a larger chunk of the planet earth. How will you ever know what it feels like to experience new adventures if you don't choose to try out what's available to you? A teacher told me recently that she lived a narrow, shallow life until her husband died. Now she travels around different parts of the world during June, July, and August during school summer recess. She feels alive for the first time.

The next time you plan a trip, choose to travel to a country where you've never been, where you don't speak the language, where you don't know anyone. Life is too precious, too short, to be redundant. If you have a job opportunity to move to Arizona, leave Ohio and go experience the mountains, the opportunity to go camping, to have a boat, to water-ski, fish, and sail. Someone in every family is the first to move away. When my brother Powell left New York to accept a job in Chicago to work for an advertising agency, I teased him, accusing him of trying to get away from our strong mother. He always denied this—with a wink and a smile.

My parents didn't travel much when I was growing up. When my father's older sister took my sister, a cousin, and me around the world in 1959, she was considered by everyone in the close-knit community of Westport, Connecticut, to be an eccentric. My aunt dared to be herself. She rejected an offer to marry a dull dentist from Philadelphia, where she would be "secure." The world was her home. She embraced it all. She was way ahead of her time. Whereas the world thought in terms of separate countries, she understood global unity and interconnection. All the narrow prejudiced views that small communities nourish vanished in her eyes. By traveling around the world, Aunt Betty became one with the world, never fitting into the narrow framework of the views of her siblings and family.

We are an expression of our exposure. When we expand our environment, we enlarge our soul. We become more seaworthy by going out to sea, by exploring the unknown, by charting new emotional territory. We get life lessons from living life fully. Push yourself to great new challenges. Choose to think originally and keep an open mind and heart. Reach out for the new, exciting adventure in order to know firsthand how you feel. The mountain peak is there; experience it. Leave the bondage of the known to awaken to the freedom of the boundless. A widow from a small town in North Carolina is reaching out in all directions to expand the life that had once been so sheltered, so safe, so limited. She's now traveling around the country, visiting with friends, going to college reunions, and taking group trips to Europe and Asia, bringing along some grandchildren.

You can leave the safe harbor in small ways every day: choose to go to a new art gallery or try a new restaurant or a new dish. Dare to dress differently from how you are used to dressing or the way your family and friends expect you to dress. Question everything you're thinking and doing. If you love color passionately, don't wear drab neutral colors after Labor Day just because this is the "proper" thing to do. Did you know that the reason for the forced march to switch our color wardrobes is so the fashion world will make more money?

Young college students today are often invited to take a junior semester or year abroad. Some agonize over these opportunities and choices and end up back at school, having declined the program because they were afraid of what they'd miss while they were away. They thought they'd miss their safe harbor, but how did they really know what they were missing? It's hard to guide a teenager into looking at the big picture when it is entirely unfamiliar, but whenever we're given an opportunity to broaden our horizons, it is always good to reach out for the new, different cultural experience.

The winter of 2004 was not our turn to spend Christmas in Washington with the grandchildren; we'd been there for Thanksgiving. Suddenly, Peter and I saw an opening, a time when we could go to Hong Kong, a dream we'd had for years. I first went to this exciting city in 1959 and returned in 1980 on a buying trip as a guest of the Singapore government. Peter had business in China and we went to Hong Kong together during that trip in the late 80s. We longed to return, to take the colorful ferry back and forth from Kowloon peninsula to Hong Kong, to be among these gentle people and experience extraordinary gourmet food throughout the region.

We left the safe harbor of New York and Stonington Village and flew nonstop to Hong Kong. For ten days we absorbed the colors, the flavors, and textures of the city. On Christmas Eve we walked from our hotel to the cultural center to enjoy the ballet *Nutcracker,* a favorite we so enjoyed with Alexandra and Brooke when they were young. Hong Kong buildings are lit up during the holiday. We found favorite spots to listen to choirs sing in hotel lobbies, to explore the magnificent holiday decorations, and to meet and enter into interesting conversations with fellow travelers, people from every corner of the globe.

Every evening we'd see the light show and fireworks with different people. It was a fascinating experience; we knew no one and yet we felt we were at a huge party with wonderful people. On December 26, the tsunami hit. So many places I'd visited when I traveled around the world with my Aunt Betty and later on my buying trip for the Singapore government were devastated by the natural tragedy.

All the memories of travel in Asia awakened in me the reality that my life has been shaped and formed by what I've seen and experienced on exotic trips to far-off places. When I was an interior designer working for Mrs. Brown's firm, McMillen, Inc., in New York, the interior designers were strongly encouraged to travel to Europe yearly to absorb the scale and proportion of Palladian architecture north of Venice, to awaken our appreciation of classic architecture and design.

Whether you leave the safe harbor of your small town and take a trip to a nearby city, or you plan to take a cruise ship from a city to a far-off beautiful island, reach out to a larger view of the world. Discover firsthand a love and appreciation for the people, the culture, the cuisine, and the natural and man-made beauty of new places. Learn other customs and rituals and participate in native celebrations, dance, and feasts.

The earth is the fifth largest planet in the solar system. There are 57.5 million square miles of dry land and 139.5 million square miles of ocean.

There are exciting places for us to go. Choose to expand your horizons by leaving behind everything that is familiar. Be a guest in an unfamiliar city or country or island. Choose to make your home more of the planet earth. It's there. Accept the invitation and go. The good life, as we discover when we travel, can be found in many places. Expand your awareness of how good people are everywhere you go when you leave the safe harbor.

Be bold and brave. Be the eccentric one in your family. What Aunt Betty did for me when I was sixteen transformed my life. She was true to her choice to explore the world. By bringing her three oldest nieces on a world trip, her gift continues to grow by making me more sensitive to the larger family of fellow human beings who share this planet.

Leave the safe harbor. Be an Aunt Betty. Take a niece or a grandchild around the world. Start a travel fund. By being daring and taking a chance, you will be embracing a wonderful way of finding happiness and joy otherwise overlooked and denied.

Sail with the wind out into the ocean of life
for an exciting voyage full of surprises, obstacles—and joy.

PETER MEGARGEE BROWN

Who Knows, It Might Be Good

It is under the greatest adversity that there exists the greatest potential for doing good, both for oneself and others.

THE DALAI LAMA

I don't know anyone who hasn't lived through difficult times. Pain and loss are central parts of the human condition. However, when something that can be considered dreadful or extremely unfortunate happens to you or to a loved one, you will find some unexpected benefits that will come out of it. Terrible things happen. I don't know why bad things happen to good and innocent people. I just accept that they do, because I experience people going through unbelievably hard times. I'm amazed how they're able to grow stronger and can inspire us by their bravery and strength of character.

Several years ago the spiritual leader Eric Butterworth returned to lead a Unity service at Lincoln Center in Manhattan. He'd had an operation and had been in a rehabilitation center for several months. Upon his return he was noticeably frail. He approached the stage in a wheelchair. Everyone gave him an extended standing ovation. Eric, in his usual teaching manner, smiled, thanked the devoted crowd, and said, "This has been a great growth period for me." While his students laughed in relief, he was quite serious. One of his favorite sayings was *Grow or Go!*

When something terrible or disappointing happens to us, we have a tendency to feel alone; we are certain no one else understands how painful is our loss. The truth is, everyone we know has to face challenging situations. We may not know the specifics, but we're all experiencing difficulties. When you go through your greatest adversity, it will make you more humble, more aware of the pain of others.

Eric Butterworth was a superb teacher of truth. He was a tough teacher because he urged his followers to believe in core principles with no exception. Truth points to the good—what is virtuous and right. When we have a sick child or are seriously ill ourselves, this is the truth. When we face it head on, when we grow through it, we will experience some sense of meaning or significance. When we go through tough times, we have a choice to grow through them.

I'll never forget the letter my mother wrote me with her signature green ink from her hospital bed several weeks before she died. Mother wrote, "It is worth having cancer and dying in order to be this close to you, Sandie darling." Study after study shows that people who experience cancer reappraise their lives in beneficial ways.

Women who found meaning in having breast cancer are better psychologically adjusted. Men who perceive benefits from having a heart attack are less likely to have a subsequent attack. They learn behavior moderation, take the appropriate medication, and are less driven by their ultra competitive, Type A tendencies.

The ability to find meaning and purpose in their suffering was essential for the survival of concentration camp prisoners. In his book *Man's Search for Meaning*, Viktor Frankl wrote about his own experience and his escape from a concentration camp. He noted how important it was "to choose one's attitude in any given set of circumstances, to choose one's own way." When someone holds a core belief that no one can take their soul, they're far more likely to survive. When people make meaning of these dreadful experiences, they're able to adjust successfully in their new condition and continue to find meaning in it. We don't choose these times when we are brought to our knees, but they can spur us to mobilize courage and inner forces of good.

Christopher Reeve is such a hero to so many of us. He said, "I think a hero is an ordinary individual who finds strength to persevere and endure in spite of overwhelming obstacles." His Holiness the Dalai Lama believes that every event, every experience that we are exposed to, comes as a kind of learning experience.

I met a ninety-year-old doctor at a wedding who is writing a book about his World War II experiences as a volunteer. He told me about how awful the war experience was. Then he smiled and said, "But Alexandra, there was a silver lining. I was twenty-eight years old and I found love. I married a nurse and we had thirty-six years together before she died."

A friend had a leg operation and was in traction in a hospital bed. When I went to visit him, Ken was reading *War and Peace* by the genius Leo Tolstoy. "I needed to be planted in one place in order to read this great book." He was always too busy working to be able to spend real time during the day reading. When we experience growth periods, it makes us more compassionate, more understanding of what others endure every day. This inner growth is a time to learn acceptance of everything that comes to us outside of our will or choice.

You can choose to improve other parts of your life while you're healing. You may have more time to read, to think, and to contemplate. If you can't go to work, you can spend more time in the garden with your wife and grandchildren. People brought so many pretty flower bouquets to a friend she was inspired to take up painting watercolors and created beautiful botanicals. We choose to accept what we cannot change and instead change our inner spirit, learning whatever there is to be learned.

The ninetheenth-century clergyman and newspaper editor, Henry Ward Beecher, wrote, "The little troubles and worries of life, so many of which we meet, may be as stumbling blocks in our way, or we may make them stepping stones to a noble character." Look for the blessing. Look for the good. Grow through your biggest challenges. Choose to make sense and meaning out of the obstacles you face. Your inner resources are extraordinary. The strength is there. Draw upon your spirit as you look at the big picture.

We can seek out the silver lining. After an illness, make some resolutions about your behavior in order to live a healthier, more balanced life. After a fire, you can choose to rebuild, relocate, rethink your home and how it works. After your spouse dies, you can sell the house and move into a condominium closer to the grandchildren. After a serious automobile accident that requires you to have daily physical therapy, you discover an opportunity to pursue a health regime career helping others to heal. Look for the blessings in disguise. Silver linings can bring lighter, brighter days after the setbacks, the losses, and the troubles. You're given an opportunity to see life from a different angle, from a richer, deeper perspective.

Love of truth shows itself in this, that a man knows how to find and value the good in everything.

GOETHE

15

Redefine What Is Beautiful

The good is the beautiful.

PLATO

It is in the small acts of our intimate, private, everyday lives that we experience the beautiful. When we create little moments that are pleasing to our senses, especially our eyes, we elevate the ordinary to the extraordinary. There's more fun and pleasure in everything we choose to do when our senses are delighted.

It certainly makes sense to focus our attention on the 95 percent of our lives that constitutes the everyday. The life we can make beautiful is the one right before us: in our home, with our family, in the yard with a small garden, in the kitchen, cooking and sharing a meal. The beautiful life is the good life. What is good is beautiful. What is beautiful is the greatest good. Beauty is the supreme good.

Why is it important to live a beautiful life? Why is it ideal to live a good life? Is there another, better way to live our lives? What is your vision of the ideal way to live? How can you apply your ideals to the life you are now living?

We experience pleasure whenever we behold beauty. When I was young, raising Alexandra and Brooke, I intuitively knew I needed beauty in order to enjoy everything more. Through the harmony of form and color, everything becomes more pleasant, more sensuous, and more appealing. A parent might not love changing a diaper, but when there is a vase of roses on a nearby table, we're reminded of why we do what we do. Beauty helps keep us from becoming overwhelmed or discouraged.

How would you define what is beautiful to your eyes, your senses, and your heart? Would your list include the beauty and colors from nature, a sunset over Stonington Village harbor, a double rainbow in Denver, Colorado, with the snow-capped Rockies in the background, a beautiful garden, a pretty painting, a couple in love, a child's smile, the first flowers of spring? What excites you aesthetically? What do you most admire? What kinds of beauty do you desire? How can beauty help you now? Has your definition of a beautiful life changed over the years? We evolve into an inner knowing of what is beautiful to us. Beauty, I believe, is a way of structuring our lives. How do you seek it out? Where do you go for inspiration, for rejuvenation?

I'm a passionate believer in the principle that order precedes beauty. We can't see and appreciate all the beauty around us if everything is a mess. We're not free to jump in and have fun if we are not organized. We can't spontaneously try out a new recipe if our counters are cluttered and the pots are dirty. We can't start a craft project if our desk or work table is heaped with papers to be filed, or elements of the last project, nor can we set a romantic dinner table for two when mail and bills are strewn around. Best to clear as you go. When we move toward greater awareness of what is beautiful, we get prepared. We put our life in order because we choose to live beautifully. When we're set up to live fully and well, all the aesthetic experiences we have will help reduce stress and inspire greater clarity of vision.

When I'm in need of more beauty, I'm instinctively drawn to nature. Nature has always been my inspiration for my interior design work. I prefer colors from the sky, water, sun, gardens, trees, and beach. I look up at the stars, the moon, the sun (both rising and setting). I go for a walk in the woods or stroll in a park. I linger on a beach or sit in front of a waterfall. I walk through as many gardens as I can discover. We should pay attention to the weather, experiencing as many sights and natural phenomena as possible. I actively look for rainbows after a rain. Claude Monet, my favorite Impressionist, understood: "Nature does not stand still . . . Nature is the most discerning guide, if one submits oneself completely to it, but when it disagrees with you, all is finished. One cannot fight nature." The more time I spend communing in natural beauty, the more receptive I am to creating a more attractive life for others and myself.

Let nature guide you. Choose to accept her sense of beauty and timing. The more natural beauty you expose yourself to, the more beauty you will feel in your heart. Some people can't absorb all the delicate natural beauty without wanting to share it through self-expression. Claude Monet painted glorious pictures. A friend who worships nature has taken up watercolor painting and has become quite skilled at rendering light and colors. Others write about nature's miraculous beauty and become poets who urge us to live beautifully with a poetic, romantic spirit. Let nature be your muse. If you ever feel confused or stuck, or you don't know what choices to make, leave your office, leave your house, leave your chores, and go outside in search of something beautiful. Make a mental note of what you see. This will have a profound effect on your perspective, mood, and attitude. I make it a habit to find greater meaning and value in my life by identifying the beauty I see in nature every day. If you spend too much time at the computer, or too much time in meetings, and struggle to catch up with your workload, it's easy to become stale, confused, and lose your insight. Go out and see for yourself how miraculously beautiful nature is. You'll be able to soak it all in and return to your work refreshed.

Last summer I moved my work downstairs to our small study from my cozy Zen writing room in the back of the cottage because I wanted to be closer to nature. The blue hydrangea were so glorious in the backyard, the roses had never been more beautiful, and even the dry, hot July and August sun didn't keep the geraniums from blooming in all the window boxes. All of this inspires me. From the one window in this small room, I'm able to see the harbor with the sailboats, small yachts, and fishing boats called draggers.

A house across the street is painted cornflower blue. In the evening, as the sun begins to set, the north side of our friend's house becomes transformed to the most heavenly violet hue. It is alive with light and energy. I leave my desk and run out to greet the sunset. This habit has left an indelible impression on me. I'm tipped off to when the sun is setting because of the light on their house. It is a spiritual pleasure for me to wonder about the mystery of it all. Why was I born? What am I on this planet earth? What am I to do with all this beauty? How can I add something to what nature so openly and generously provides for us? How can I stay awake to and aware of her wonders?

In 2004 when I taught a four-day workshop at Omega Institute on the subject of my book *Living a Beautiful Life*, we agreed that we can't seek, see, experience, or create beauty unless we're happy. We could be in paradise, but if we aren't happy, we wouldn't be aware of our blessings. We can live in a beautiful house with a lovely garden, but if we're unhappy, we don't experience the beauty all around us. Beauty, like love, makes us happy, but we have to be keenly receptive to the seduction.

Until I went to New York City to study interior design, I had a natural sense of what was beautiful. Then I lost my aesthetic voice. I was sixteen, deeply impressionable, and slipped into mimicking the point of view of my professors. This temporarily threw me off my path. I was also star struck. The charming legendary interior decorator, Billy Baldwin, for example, was a friend of Eleanor McMillen Brown, my mentor and boss. She generously invited her young designers to dinner with the famous, established ones. I adored Billy Baldwin from the moment we met. I wasn't alone; lots of young designers tried to copy him even though we all knew imitation is deadly.

I got swept up in New York sophistication and made many mistakes. When I was faced with a long, narrow hallway in my apartment on Sixty-fifth Street between Madison and Fifth Avenue in Manhattan, I thought it would be chic to lacquer the walls chocolate brown. To make matters worse, my current boss loved leopard designs—the rage in the 60s. I had leopard print wall-to-wall carpet installed in this "great" hall. Then I went even farther off base and had cut crystal ceiling light fixtures installed. By any standard, it was vulgar, dark, pretentious, inappropriate, and tacky. Can you just imagine my beautiful blond daughters crawling around this space with their toys, their dolls, and their teddy bears? It's amazing they don't suffer from seasonal affective disorder from lack of light! I was seriously "other-directed" in my interior design disaster that "everyone" admired. It wasn't *me* and it wasn't beautiful to *me*. The laundry room doubled as a room for our live-in helper and was fresh white with cheerful bright Marimekko fabric on the daybed and pillows. Alexandra and Brooke were naturally drawn to the light. We all congregated in this cheerful, cute little space where plants thrived and so did we.

I've learned to trust my inner voice in what I find to be beautiful. I like light, bright, cheerful background colors for oil paintings. Watercolors on white paper please my eye. Rembrandt was a great artist, but his dark backgrounds bring a tinge of sadness to my soul. Dark art is dreary to me. I've bought art with dark backgrounds, but these aesthetic missteps now sit in the back of a closet.

My favorite contemporary artist, Roger Mühl, has become a friend over these past forty-five years. He often tells me that he can't paint if he is unhappy. He paints out of exuberance, a love of life, a joy in color and light, in nature, in beauty. He loves beauty so much; he understands that it is precious, even fragile. Mühl and Claude Monet share a gift of showing us just how beautiful our lives really are, right here, right now, down to the folds in the white tablecloth, the Brie cheese ripe on a dish, the child underfoot at play.

Discover and rediscover new habits of finding and expressing beauty. Perhaps you will make more trips to a nearby botanical garden or art museum, or spend more time enjoying the beauty of a local park. Try to leave enough time to take the scenic route to work. Take time to savor the beauty of the fruit and vegetable displays at the local market. Photograph your newfound beauty. Keep a beauty scrapbook. What could be more revealing? When you focus on beauty, you will become happier. This enterprise will turn up new definitions of beauty.

What is considered beautiful to someone else may be ugly to our eyes. Be true to your own vision. Then you're free to become influenced by others' sense of beauty when it is authentically yours as well. Absorb as much as you can from people with whom you share a finely attuned aesthetic.

What is beautiful to all your five senses and beyond? Some opinionated people have a narrow concept of what is beautiful; they only like classical painting or eighteenth-century porcelains, for example. Redefining what is beautiful broadens our appreciation for all different kinds of beauty. We should become more receptive to drawing inspiration from the expansive variety of the entire world, not just from our limited exposure and knowledge.

What is beautiful to you now? What is beautiful literature to you? What kind of poetry do you find beautiful? Keep a running list of all the different areas in your life that you find most beautiful. You will see clearly that you experience beauty everywhere. Don't you find beauty in architecture, color, learning, music, love, children, and home?

In the various areas of your life, reevaluate and redefine what is beautiful to you. Our taste is refined as we become more sensitive to the nuances of scale, proportion, symmetry, color, and light. We develop an eye for beauty as we learn to express ourselves more honestly. We see the beauty in something well made by a caring hand. We feel the energy of things that are harmoniously placed in a room, a garden, or a city. We see the beauty in a well-made house, chair, or table, well-made suit or well-tailored shirt, a well-sung song, a well-written story well told.

Seek to make fresh discoveries of what you now believe to be most beautiful. Be willing to make big life changes in order to give your life greater form and meaning. Choose to recommit yourself to living a beautiful life in your thoughts and in your acts of self-expression.

Every day look at a beautiful picture, read a beautiful poem, listen to some beautiful music, and if possible, say some reasonable thing.

GOETHE

The Power of Flowers

We should enjoy this summer, flower by flower,
as if it were to be the last one we'll see.

ANDRÉ GIDE

When I think of beauty, when I envision the good life, flowers immediately come to mind. They have a powerful hold over our spirit and never fail to uplift us. I have made the bold choice to never live a day without fresh flowers or blossoming plants. A part of me would die inside if I couldn't gaze at their delicate beauty, smell their aroma, and let their colors charm me. I choose to spend money on what some might consider an extravagance. I must be true to my commitment to flowers in order to live a good life.

The Buddha envisioned the universe turning into a bouquet of flowers at the hour of his enlightenment. Because my earliest memory is of being surrounded by color in my mother's flower garden, I have a strong feeling that my soul is nurtured by my passion for flowers. The garden is my metaphor for living well, creating paradise on earth by cultivating a garden. The beauty of flowers makes life so much more beautiful, more sacred, more intensely alive.

Our brain chemistry changes when we're in natural beauty. The rejuvenating power of nature is well known. I'm glad to see hospitals having healing gardens, where the patients can water and prune and walk among the beauty. Flowers are there for us all on the happiest days of our lives, as well as at the saddest times. Flowers have kept me company during the most difficult times of great pain and loss as silent witnesses to the mysteries of life, the power of love. Flowers respond to our tenderness and care. I talk to flowers as I prune and arrange them. I let them know how much pleasure they bring me. Flowers speak to us by blooming, opening up their buds to colorful blossoms. Antoine de Saint-Exupéry said, "It is the time you have wasted for your rose that makes your rose so important."

Flowers are a great gift to our sense of sight, our sense of smell, and our sense of touch. We eat some flowers in salads and soups. My favorite tea is jasmine. Flowers call to us, they speak a language we can almost hear.

In a vase, flowers sing in a chorus of colorful grace notes, quivering in the breeze by an open window. Flowers provide accents of temporary color in a room. In a garden the colors seem to draw us in; we come to greet the new lily blooming. The first flower mentioned in literature is the lotus, the flowering water lily, a favorite of Claude Monet. Through his paintings of water lilies and the lilies in his pond at his glorious gardens in Giverny, he helped teach me to look into the depth of things, to expand my perspective rather than observing just the surface: "I have always loved the sky and the water, greenery, flowers. All these elements were to be found in abundance here in my little pond."

Monet was a passionate gardener. He loved nature so much he created in Giverny a magnificent corner of the universe. He once said, "I'm good for two things, painting and gardening." If you haven't been to his house and gardens, I urge you to make the pilgrimage. He once told a friend, "Everything I have earned has gone into these gardens. I do not deny that I am proud of them. I am very happy, very enchanted . . . for I am surrounded here by everything I love . . . My desire would be to stay just like this forever, in a quiet corner of nature."

Do you have a favorite flower? Do you have several favorites? Are there some flowers that have a strong hold over you? Do you have a sentimental feeling about certain flowers? What are some of your favorite scents? I carried lily-of-the-valley on my wedding day when Peter and I were married. Alexandra and Brooke carried bouquets of lily-of-the-valley and wore halos of this delicate fragrant bellflower. I have a granddaughter named Lily.

We should accept the invitation to live with and appreciate flowers every day. Flower children wear flowers to symbolize peace and love. Flowers symbolize perfect truth and purity. The Chinese and Japanese especially find significance in flowers. The Japanese saw the transcience of life in the cherry blossom. The ancient art of flower arranging continues to add meaning to our lives today when we create a small bouquet for a kitchen table.

Leonardo da Vinci always had flowers around him. He loved the scent. He believed the five senses are the ministers of the soul. He talked about the synergy of the senses—a great secret of great artists and scientists. Of a garden, he exclaimed, "Who would believe that so small a space could contain the images of the whole universe."

Last year I was a judge at the San Francisco garden show. While I was off judging with two expert gardeners, Peter was quietly walking about on his own. Several hours later when our choices were made, I went to greet Peter, who had a sweet grin on his face. He kissed me and said, "Flowers are the most exquisite thing I can think of right now . . . ," and then he kissed me again, "besides you." He showed me a small pocket-sized spiral notebook where he'd jotted down some notes. With his permission, let me share a few of them with you:

* To sit serenely in a garden in unconscious meditation lifts us into another world of reflection, contemplation, and love. A moment's peace.

* The garden sings of beauty and truth with all the complexity and simplicity of natural divine design.

* Come walk slowly in the gardens and be at peace.

* Flowers create beauty and happiness where there is none.

* Every soul can have a flower to inspire and enhance the richness of our day—but few understand.

* Flowers have a special channel to romance, health, and love.
* In choosing happiness, choose your flower, then your garden.
* Better to be a gardener than own a garden.
* Flowers celebrate the day.

Try to have a small arrangement of flowers by your bed. One single flower will give you the same sensuous sweetness as a bouquet and will remind you that you cannot create a flower but you can plant seeds and be a co-creator. Add floral fabrics to your rooms in the upholstery and curtains, as well as bed covers, sheets, tablecloths, and napkins. Hang botanical watercolors on the wall. Select china with flower designs. Let the sheer beauty of flowers delight you, lift your spirits, and allow you to create an enchanted garden right where you are. Flowers are fragile. They are impermanent as all things are. Take time to enjoy them completely. Be there to appreciate your flowers and tend to them when they're in bloom.

.　.　.

There was a cute story in Kay Redfield Jamison's enthusiastic book *Exuberance: The Passion for Life*. She quoted Eric Hanson's book *Orchid Fever,* in which he interviewed an orchid grower who had started with a single windowsill plant. "Pretty soon, I decided I wanted another orchid. First a red one, then a pink one, then I had to have a white one with spots . . . I couldn't stop . . . now I have a 2,200 square foot greenhouse with 200,000 orchid plants!"

Jamison writes of another enthusiast who talked about how his first wife couldn't handle his obsession: "One morning she sat him down at the breakfast table and explained that he would have to choose between his orchid collection and their marriage. 'That's the easiest decision I'll ever make,' he told her. 'You're out of here, baby!'"

I'm lucky enough to be married to a tender, gentle soul who loves every new bud on our rose bushes, every new blooming geranium blossom. Peter and I sit in our tiny backyard surrounded by Nikko blue hydrangea in an ecstatic trance of love and gratitude for the flowers that cheer us along. We renew ourselves each day through their magical beauty and grace.

Plant seeds, water, weed, prune, fertilize. Take time to grow roses. Take time to smell the roses. Look and really see the miracle of creation in a single flower.

> Flowers are the living food of the spirit;
> they are the symbol of life itself.
>
> **CHARLES MASSON**

Share the Beauty

There's no delight in owning anything unshared.

SENECA

Life is made up of simple little gestures of goodwill. Without them, we would be impoverished. I remember with such delight a retired Episcopal minister who lives down the street from us in Stonington Village, who five years ago dropped off a beautiful soft pink rose with a ribbon and a card that said, "Congratulations, Granny," when he learned of the twins' birth. Raymond didn't sign the card so I wasn't sure whom to thank. Having it be a secret surprise sweetened the kind thought and gift.

A friend and fellow wine lover tasted some delicious white wine from France and bought a case for his restaurant. He brought us a bottle with a sprig of lilac from his trees tied around it. The extra flourish of the perfume of the lilac brought us such happiness. For whatever reason, our lilac trees hadn't blossomed yet, so it was a treat of pleasure as well as one of anticipation of the glorious lilac trees in bloom.

We knew the wine was much too fine not to share with friends, so we invited ourselves to go across the street to Mary Ellen and Rick's house to watch a spectacular sunset on their terrace. We toasted our mutual friend John, thankful for the special treat.

I love to be remembered when friends go on a vacation and bring me a small gift, one that is local to where they traveled. This is a wonderful way for us to envision being there, especially if the place is familiar to us or one of our favorite spots. Our daughter Brooke travels to Paris often on business as well as for pleasure and never fails to bring us back some art postcards, cocktail napkins, perfumed soap, or paper products we've grown to love.

When a friend's garden is crammed with roses, we're often given a bouquet. On Saturday mornings in the summer and fall, we have a ritual of going to the farmers' market down the street. We often pick up some extra berries or peaches or whatever is in season to bring to a friend when we go for a glass of wine or for supper.

If daffodils are in bloom in your yard, you can bring a bunch in an inexpensive glass container to a restaurant and leave them for other customers to appreciate. If you have baked a batch of sugar cookies, you can bring a few in a colorful napkin tied with a pretty ribbon to give to a bank teller, a post office worker, or a friend who works in a nearby gift store.

I love to see other people's gardens. I understand the joy of having an enchanting private garden in the back of a house, but it is also so nice to have flowers in the front yard or in window boxes for neighbors to enjoy as well. A woman whom I do not know apparently admired our roses on her daily walks by our cottage. Inspired, she took some wonderful photographs of them and handed them to Peter when he was picking up his newspaper at the newsstand. No name on the envelope. It isn't necessary to be thanked for everything. She was happy just to see and smell our roses. Now I have some wonderful photographs of them from a thoughtful lady who enjoys them as much as we do.

I carry several pretty postcards with me, usually a ribbon bookmark or two, and a Mother Teresa poem printed on a card. You never know who you'll meet who might need a lift. Children always love the ribbons.

It's so wonderful when friends send us pictures from their travels, photographs of their children, their houses, and their gardens. I adore receiving a handwritten note on a pretty floral card or a reproduction of a favorite Impressionist painting. When someone hears music they think

I'll enjoy, I'm grateful to be introduced to new sounds by someone who is more musical than I am. In the same way, I'm always so grateful when a fan or friend tells me about a book they think I'd enjoy reading. I can't count how many times people send me tea bags enclosed with a note, introducing me to a new favorite flavor.

Share the beauty with those around you. I'm convinced that the more we share, the more abundantly alive we feel. Sharing deepens our sense of belonging, of inner connection, and of being loved.

And those are the two things, tenderness and beauty.

D. H. LAWRENCE

18

Live with the Objects You Love

What we love we grow to resemble.

SAINT BERNARD

The treasured things we select to live with are so deeply personal and so meaningful that they are the material echo of our heart and our soul. Objects we collect are strong symbols, reminders of expansive experiences that evoke strong memories. I'm a great believer in expressing sentimental, nostalgic feelings through the tangible things we gather to live with at home.

Your home can't be too personal. We all want to know more about the interests, adventures, and passions of loved ones through the unusual, colorful, meaningful objects they collect over their lifetimes. What you love gives you a sense of spirit of place, a feeling of belonging, of home. You're among friends. You miss your treasures when you're away. Things you love raise your spirits when you return home. They welcome you as reminders of who you are, who you were, and who you are becoming.

When you love something, there is a reason why. You may have an interesting story behind how you came to discover it, how you reacted, how you came to love it. It really doesn't matter what the object is—it could be a painting, an old piece of crystal, or a hand-hooked rug. If you acquired a quilt or a hand-blown vase or a writing desk because it touched your soul, if it means a lot to you regardless of its market value, it was meant to be. When you bring home and live with objects, you are touched by mysterious connections between you and the maker of something that you find beautiful.

Whenever I've fallen in love with something, I usually have vivid memories of the beautiful experience that surrounded the moment of discovery. You can put something you love here or there. Chances are the object you love will not end up where you thought it would. You feel the warmth of the presence of this special item no matter where you decide to put it.

I remember when a woman begged me to sell her a small painting by Roger Mühl that was resting on an easel on our mantel in our living room. She was totally in love with this picture of a sun-drenched cottage in Provence by the Mediterranean Sea. I held the painting in my hands. On the back was a note from Peter who'd given this to me as a gift at one of the artist's openings. I opened the envelope and read his words; tears streamed down my cheeks. There was no way I could part with this painting. When we love something deeply, and it was a gift from our love, it is a double blessing to be able to live with it.

When you look around other people's houses, you will observe things that are meaningful to them. What are the characteristics of the things that enlighten and inspire your soul? What draws you to a French provincial table or an old patchwork quilt or a particular work of art? Studying the objects you love deepens their beauty and illuminating power.

If you purchase something while you are on a romantic trip with your spouse or if you're on a family vacation and your children help you select the object, you will have a strong attachment to this object that you may never outgrow. I see this so often as an interior designer. I ask a client about the significance of an item and I hear an outpouring of emotion.

A useful exercise is to go to a neutral place where you are not near any of your treasures. Make a list—stream of consciousness—of all the things you most adore, including a favorite jacket or bracelet or photograph album or antique chair. Mentally scan your rooms and closets, trying to visualize all of the objects you most love. You will find, by writing down a wide range of objects, that certain items are of key importance to you.

What are some of your treasured objects you most love? Why do you have such a strong attachment to them? What do they represent that is intangible and invisible? The Buddha instructs that we have to give up our attachments to things in order not to suffer. This is true. I feel we suffer, however, when we are not connected to objects of our desire, the favorite things we've grown to love and adore. To have never had the opportunity or the privilege to live with objects that are beautiful, meaningful, and good for us is to suffer.

While we're still here on this physical plane, let us celebrate all the amazing beauty that is available to us. So many of the objects of our affection offer a mysterious connection between the resources of nature and man's impulse to create something original. The things you love are not on display or for show. They are private intimate connections to amazing experiences in all parts of the globe, to loved ones who know what you adore, and to a strange and wonderful connection you and I have to certain things that speak to us and for us. The objects we adore are made from human energy and spirit. When the energy is good, the object is good and good for you. Let me list a few of the objects I love:

* Books written by literary friends of all ages that I've read, reread, and refer to year after year.

* Family memorabilia that reintroduce me to other family members— alive and dead—who are part of my personal story, my autobiography.

* Framed photographs or gifts given to me by friends who have died.

* Because of my passion for flowers, I'm enormously attracted to flower containers of all sorts and sizes, including cachepots for plants. I love the patina of an old terra cotta pot covered with green fungi that makes it mellow and charming.

* Peter and I collect brass weights that are old and practical and have

been used for years. We also enjoy brass scales that are beautiful in their function and remind us of honesty, balance, and justice.

* We love bells and have them around different rooms to ring randomly.

* Our collection of botanical watercolors that we appreciate flower by flower.

* When I married Peter, he had a collection of nineteenth-century carriage clocks I've grown to love. The one we have in our bedroom makes the most incredible bong on the hour. There is a remarkable throb of tone that reverberates through the room. I feel it is expressing exuberance, a wow.

* Paperweights are light catching, have sparkle, and many of mine have color. They're reminiscent of several wonderful trips to Murano near Venice, where they're made, and are useful on my writing desk.

* My pens are as important to me as an artist's brushes. I have many and use them all. There is something profoundly satisfying to have just the right pen with flowing ink.

* I have three favorite writing desks—they are all old, they all have a story behind them, and I feel they have great energy.

What are some of your favorite treasures? What do you value and love that tells a story and that you don't want to part with until you die? I remember in the early 60s falling in love with two primitive ceramic dolls while on vacation in Greece. I can't tell you now or perhaps ever why they spoke to me and still do all these years later, but they do. There is something about this pair of male and female ceramic dolls that speaks to my essence. My soul is involved. They cost eight dollars and are priceless.

Choose to live with things you love. Refuse to live with things you don't need, want, or desire. There is no point. Life is fragile and short. Be sure you are the caregiver to objects you truly love. There is a lot of stuff out there and it is just stuff. Far better to weed things out so you have fewer but more favorite things around to use and enjoy. Be true to your heart by surrounding yourself with things that have great meaning, that are representative of your spirit. There are so many people who aren't able to live with objects they love. Reach out to these souls. We have to constantly remind ourselves just how fortunate we are.

> The meaning of things lies not in the things
> themselves but in our attitude toward them.
>
> **ANTOINE DE SAINT-EXUPÉRY**

19

Why Not Be Comfortable?

Must we always talk for victory, and never once for truth,
for comfort, and joy?

EMERSON

Common sense tells us that we should choose to be comfortable, but so often we forget how important comfort is. When we have good health, we tend to take it for granted. The same seems true of creature comforts. When we feel comfortable, in tangible as well as intangible ways, we should pay attention to the elements that make us feel so well environmentally and physiologically, as well as spiritually.

While many of us live with some kind of bodily discomfort and pain, we should try not to add to the problem by ignoring our need for comfort. About twenty years ago, while in Spain on a family vacation, I found some chartreuse patterned leather flats. I can't remember that they were too tight or that I hobbled around Madrid in pain, but years later, I pulled these shoes out of my closet, dusted them off, and put them on to coordinate with my chartreuse slacks. Ouch. My right foot is a good half size larger than my left. Ouch. Ouch. My feet have grown larger now that I am wearing more comfortable soft leather shoes. But I was in denial. Dumb as I was, I thought, "If the shoe doesn't fit, wear it." I lived through a painful day of my feet aching so badly I wanted to cry. I wasn't at the beach where I could kick off my shoes; I was in New York City, going from place to place, meeting to meeting. You could see the pain on my face. If you have blisters on your heel, you can't think lofty thoughts. We choose ouch vs. ahh.

Our foot doctor told Peter and me that a large portion of the operations he performs are on women who have damaged their feet by their choice of footwear. "Try telling a thirty-five-year-old woman to wear sensible shoes . . . she won't listen."

For years I wore uncomfortably tight earrings because I was afraid if they were comfortable they might fall off. I got so used to the pain, I thought it was natural to be uncomfortable. My mother told me growing up that when you're not comfortable, you look more beautiful. Where did this advice come from? This is simply not true.

It amazes me the types of underpants Victoria's Secret sells to prevent lines under snug-fitting pants. Can you just imagine the discomfort? If there is a label on the back of a blouse, I remove it so it won't irritate me. The smallest thing can cause us discomfort. A blouse that is too tight and gapes at the bra line can cause a woman to slouch her shoulders, causing bad posture. If you've ever worn slacks that are too tight and they chafe, you know how it feels. It's wonderful to wear pants that are loose enough so we can move easily and freely. Our clothes are meant to serve us, to be practical and comfortable as well as stylish.

The good life is not about being Spartan. Remember, the Buddha didn't become enlightened until he sat comfortably under the bodhi tree. There is great luxury in being comfortable. Being cozy is an important part of living well. Life is made up of little comforts. Think of the comfort a child feels carrying around a security blanket or teddy bear.

Be gentle on yourself. Life is going to naturally cause us discomfort over the years, no matter what our choices. We can choose to treat ourselves tenderly in big obvious ways as well as little things to make ourselves more comfortable so that we can enjoy whatever we're doing.

Do whatever you can to add comfort at home. The best investment you can make is to have a good mattress and good comfortable upholstered furniture. I love to sit in a swivel chair where I'm free to move without having to get up.

Add a cushion to a bench. Put a wool throw blanket over your legs to feel cozy on the sofa. The legendary interior decorator, Elsie de Wolfe, believed, "The only thing that rivals the comfort of candlelight is the glow of an open fire." Many of my clients never use their fireplaces because they feel building a fire is too messy and too much work. I'd chop my own wood in a forest if I had to in order to enjoy the comfort of sitting by a fire with my feet on a footstool reading or enjoying an intimate conversation.

When you're comfortable, you're free. Why not enjoy a shag rug underfoot in your bedroom if that makes you feel good? Fold an antique quilt at the foot of the bed for emotional comfort as well as warmth when desired. Frame a picture of yourself when you were two or three years old and looked darling. That's who you are. Take comfort in *you*. Comfort allows you to meditate and contemplate without distractions. You're less tired when you feel comfortable because you're increasing your appreciation of life.

Consider the real comforts you enjoy—a small table for your dictionary so it is always right next to you at the desk. Having a footstool handy is always a grace note. I tuck a tiny, pretty, flower-covered pillow under my arm as I write. I use a pillow at the back of a chair as well as having a cushion on the seat.

When choosing art and decorative objects for your home, be sure they are easy on the eye, inviting and comfortable. Several Impressionist artists painted comfortable interiors; one of my favorites is Matisse, who wrote in *Notes of a Painter,* "What I dream of is an art of balance, of purity and serenity devoid of troubling or depressing subject matter . . . a soothing, calming influence on the mind, something like a good armchair which provides relaxation from physical fatigue."

Always consider your emotional as well as physical comfort. On a steamy August afternoon, a cool bath, a bathrobe, and a ten-minute rest in bed under a ceiling fan can be just the right choice before you get going. During heatwaves when there is no breeze and humidity is high, rather than eating out-of-doors on the water, Peter and I go to Noah's restaurant for lunch to soak in the air conditioning while enjoying a delicious meal in the luxury of comfort.

The good life softens the blows of stress and anxiety through comfort. Familiar places, an old sweater, a neck roll, smooth white paper, a good fountain pen, soft sheets, soothing music, comfortable clothes to wear, comfort food to eat, all add to greater ease of mind and body. The greatest comfort is to be comfortable with who you are, and to surround yourself with comfortable good people.

> Luxury need not have a price—comfort itself is a luxury.
>
> **GEOFFREY BEENE**

Maintain Balance Through Your Choices

Moral virtue is the habit of making right choices.

ARISTOTLE

The good life is the life that is just right for you. What is your definition of the good life? What choices do you believe you should make that will help you to establish and maintain a healthy balance throughout the course of your entire life? What plans or habits could you develop that will help you to regularly make the right choices? How can we choose to seek and acquire the things that are really good for us to have? How can we acquire the ability to discern what is right for us, aiming at every real good—in the right balance? How can we seek things that satisfy our real needs?

How can we look at the big picture, the long-range goods, and not choose the expedient narrow or self-serving interests? What are the real goods?

Our wise choices guide us into a greater realization of our capacities. We're better able to understand our own real needs and satisfy them when we choose these real goods in the right order, to the right measure, at the right time, and for the right reasons. I believe in Aristotle's doctrine of the Golden Mean: the sensible, moderate course, the middle point or ground between the too extremes of too little and too much. To achieve human happiness, we must know what is good and good for us and others and we must make our choices based on the wisdom and truth of this knowledge.

Whenever we're swayed by others or outside forces, we're off our path. Correcting the imbalance is the hard but necessary part of each right decision. There is great wisdom in striking a happy medium between the polar opposites of too little and too much. We don't always get it right, but the effort itself carries learning and meaning.

We need to adopt a sound plan, one that will guide us to our greatest good. We have to put everything in perspective, avoiding the extremes. All or nothing doesn't work. There's safety and goodness in the center. Moderation in all things.

Resist the temptation to overindulge. We're all tempted with bodily pleasures because we can have them immediately. Choose between the cookies and the ice cream. The habit of moderation enables us to resist what appears good right now in the short run in favor of what is really good for us in the long run. Perhaps you and your spouse or child could share an entrée to save calories and money when you dine out. At home you can manage portion control. The same goes for drinking wine. Shakespeare's Othello said, "Good wine is a good familiar creature, if it is well used."

We also need to seriously consider the balance between our physical and mental exercise. I know a lot of people who exercise their bodies madly in order to stay fit, to reduce stress, and to feel better physically. They seldom exercise their mind other than reading the newspaper and doing whatever their job requires of them because mental exercise requires far more discipline and hard work. At the other extreme are people who work so hard on projects or at their job that they never take time for a leisurely walk, a yoga class, or a session at the gym.

Our emotions need balance as well. By reading great literature, thinking about the "big questions," taking time to muse, and making time to be with cherished family and friends, we keep our mind-body connection in balance and create excellence at the center of our soul.

Another key area of our lives that needs careful practical wisdom is the choices we make to balance our work and leisure time. The great thought of my friend and literary agent, Carl Brandt, is, "Just because you can doesn't mean you should." This middle ground seems hardest to find. People are either too busy at the office, aiming at acquiring wealth, power, and fame at the expense of spending time with their families or doing volunteer work, or they want to have fun and they don't pay enough attention to fulfilling their deeper needs. Both extremes diminish the good life.

I smile every time I think of the essayist E. B. White, who once wrote, "I arise in the morning torn between a desire to improve (or save) the world and a desire to enjoy (or savor) the world. This makes it hard to plan the day." We acquire the skill of practical wisdom choice by choice. Practical wisdom can be applied to virtually all areas of our life with increasing success. It seems to capture the essence of this ideology of balance, not only lofty, not only of the senses, but wisdom based on reality both physical and spiritual. Study the consequences of your choices. What will this choice you make today mean down the road? Will this choice hurt others? Lao Tzu spoke practically to the people: "To go beyond is as wrong as to fall short."

We ought to try to take whatever pains are necessary to do the right thing for the sake of living a good life. Through study, meditation, visualization, relaxation, and yes, prayer, we can muster up the courage to choose what is really good. We have an obligation to make an effort not to overdo. Our good life and the lives of others depend on our assuming responsibility for living by the Golden Mean. Nothing could be more worthwhile or more satisfying. When we feel content with the balance of our lives, we have what we want and we feel happy.

Nothing to Excess.

INSCRIPTION IN THE TEMPLE OF APOLLO AT DELPHI

Cultivate Good Energy

Achieving genuine happiness may require bringing
about a transformation in your outlook, your way of thinking,
and this is not a simple matter.

THE DALAI LAMA

We all have an aura of energy. There are powerful invisible, nonmaterial forces in us that we aren't aware of. My term for this force for good in each of us is "spirit-energy." Our spirit is the breath of life, the vital principle, and the mystery inside each of us. The biggest challenge we have is to nurture, improve, and refine our life force, our energy. In order to transform ourselves, we need good, strong, productive vitality. Living the good life makes us rich, abundantly alive, able to soar. We need to use all our strength and power to live the best possible life imaginable.

No one can do this inner work for us. It's up to us to change our attitude to be more positive, to use our energy for greater good, to spread more light. What goes on externally may be beyond our power to choose, but our inner development, how we deal with our emotions, how we train and discipline our mind, is in our power.

The good news is that the brain stays changeable throughout our lives. Through training, any disturbing, wrong, inappropriate emotions can be changed to intelligent, good feelings. A Buddhist monk once told his students, "There is the possibility of transforming the undesirable into the desirable." Neuroscience teaches us we have a magic quarter of a second in which we have a crucial choice point to flip a negative, self-destructive thought into a good, life-sustaining emotion. If you look out the window in the morning and see stormy weather, before you give yourself time to say "Uh oh, this is going to be a bad day for me," flip it around and think to be sure to wear a raincoat and a smile and carry a brightly colored umbrella. When you're playing cards and think, "My opponent is cheating," focus on the reality that this is your best friend. Play your best game. If you have a thought that your boss doesn't like you and wants you fired, you may wonder if you should quit. Recall that you received a bonus last year and recently were complimented on the major project that you completed. Flip it. It is here where the energy changes and becomes more pure, more vitally alive.

There is no time in our life when we're faced with a choice-less moment. You and I continuously choose in order to cultivate good energy. Because energy is contagious, even though it is invisible its intangible quality surrounds us and creates an atmosphere. I've learned to trust my sixth sense about people and places, and it has been a tremendous help to me in my quest.

In his important book, *Emotional Intelligence*, Daniel Goleman writes, "Among the main biological changes in *happiness* is an increased activity in a brain center that inhibits negative feelings and fosters an increase in available energy." We're naturally attracted to positive energy. It directly adds to the sense of well-being, happiness, and good energy around us. Cultivating good energy is a worthwhile pursuit that is accumulative. The more we eliminate any bad thoughts that are counterproductive, the more we will be retraining our minds to choose positive over negative reactions.

In my book *Choosing Happiness: Keys to a Joyful Life,* I wrote that our natural temperament and disposition is divided evenly between nature—our genetic endowment—and nurture—the influence of our environment and our choices. We can change our life by as much as 50 percent by retraining our minds and attitudes. By thinking thoughts that aim us in the direction of greater happiness, we will, in time, transform our inner life. We're able to improve ourselves choice by choice, by our habits of thought and attitude. This character development brings rich rewards. Our mental state becomes more dependable, predictable, and stable as we cultivate good energy. When we develop this essential virtue of clarity of thinking by training and reprogramming our minds, we will live well.

Where do you choose to channel your energy? What makes you feel most alive? What inspires you to choose to do the right thing, to think the good thought? We can practice cultivating good energy in all of our real life situations, right where we are, even in tense situations. A miserable couple went to a restaurant for dinner. From the moment they sat down, they had a big chip on their shoulder. They were rude, mean, and confrontational. Karen, the waitress, told us she killed them with kindness, but it didn't work. Smiling, Karen said, "Bad vibes." They stormed out without paying. Karen kept smiling. "Good riddance."

In general, try to be more mindful of your breathing, your energy—your breath of life—especially when you are faced with a disturbing situation. Try to catch yourself thinking negative thoughts. Be mindful of your choice to replace a negative automatic reaction with a constructive thought. We expand the scope of our awareness by being totally present to what we are thinking, feeling, and observing. Be still and receptive to your attitude. There may be a lot of upsetting things happening around us and to us. Still, we choose how we are going to control ourselves, how we are going to react.

Our wise thoughts can make the world better. Bad thoughts create chaos. Choose the good-quality thought, the one that is the most helpful to you and to others. Good thinking leads to good living. The good life demands that we develop an optimistic philosophy as the framework for our thinking. We change the way we feel by what we think. The world may or may not be a good world overall, but it is possible, in fact it is vital, to make that part of the world where you live as good as it can be. If we do the things that we are capable of doing, no matter how small, the world would be a better place for us all.

> Even the most deeply implanted habits of the heart learned in childhood can be reshaped. Emotional learning is lifelong.
>
> **DANIEL GOLEMAN**

Cheap Thrills Are Thrilling

Every time you avoid buying and spending, you are saving money.

PETER MEGARGEE BROWN

It's fun to have some benefits that don't cost a bundle of money or take a lot of time. There are little grace notes available to us, but we have to be on the lookout for them because they are not always obvious.

Peter and I have made many trips to Paris, a city we adore. We were in the habit of choosing a morning flight from Paris to New York. Our theory was that we'd fly in the sunlight and be in New York in time to unpack, get settled in, and open our mail. My daughter Brooke, also a Paris devotee, suggested that we take an evening flight instead in order to gain an extra day in Paris without having to pay for the hotel room. Wow. It makes such sense. When we flew during the day, we didn't get much daylight because the plane was darkened for people who watch the movie. Daytime flights also tend to be noisy and disruptive. The evening flight is quiet, rather mellow, and provides time to read without distractions. Who is in a rush to get home from Paris? Why rush to unpack? Why hurry to get settled in? Now we leave the hotel with our bags checked in with the porter, have a leisurely lunch, and have our last stroll around Paris before we pick up our bags and go to the airport in the late afternoon. A free day in Paris is a really exciting cheap thrill.

I've now learned that the evening shuttle flights from New York to Washington, D.C., where we visit our grandchildren, have greatly reduced fares for senior citizens. We can catch a few more hours with the grandchildren, or we can enjoy Washington for some time alone together before going home. We often save money by traveling off-peak times on the train. It's less crowded and quieter, and we get better seats and enjoy the experience more.

Several years ago, we used our American Airlines miles for an all-inclusive trip to a resort in Barbados. When we checked out of the hotel, we had a zero balance on our bill. Every refreshing drink, all the great meals we enjoyed poolside or in one of the resort's several restaurants, was part of the plan. Even the ground transportation from the airport to the resort was covered. We went twice in one winter because we had so many airline miles—two free vacations in the sun in the dread cold of winter!

Peter and I enjoy going to some of the finest restaurants in New York City for celebration lunches, where we order the special of the day, a three-course meal for approximately twenty dollars—give or take a few dollars. The whole idea started years ago when the high-end restaurants wanted to fill their tables during the day. The portions are small. Perfect for healthy indulgence. The menu has several specials to choose from, plus a dessert of sorbet or fruit. If you are not in the habit of having delicious desserts on a daily basis, this is a great treat; you can share small tastes and leave the restaurant neither stuffed or broke.

When the weather is ideal, you can request a table at a restaurant on the terrace in the evening so you can dine in nature, observing the beauty of a garden or a brook or a harbor while the sun sets, at no additional cost. Seek out these great opportunities.

When we intelligently avoid excess expenditures, we feel good that we are not wasting money while we're able to enjoy some perks. I've learned, too, that it never hurts to ask a question or two in pursuit of these grace notes. A few years ago when I was giving some seminars at a home show in Naples, Florida, the manager asked me what time Peter and I wanted to fly back to New York. Not being in a rush to get back to the bitter cold and snow, I laughed and said, "Early evening." As it turned out, the beach resort where we were staying had been under renovation for months and was not full. When I asked if we could have late checkout, the answer was, "Certainly, Ms. Stoddard, what time would you like to leave?" There was no additional charge. Our room had a balcony overlooking the ocean. My eight talks were behind me. We could sit on the balcony in our terrycloth bathrobes looking at the water, talking and reading, unwinding in the privacy and luxury of time. What a gift.

When we went down to the harbor in Kowloon to take a ferry to Hong Kong, there was a long, long line of passengers on the right lane waiting to pay for their tickets. There was an empty lane on the left. As we are seniors, I inquired about any special rates for seniors. We were eligible for free ferry rides the entire ten days we were there.

Make your own list of some of your own cheap thrills to add to mine:

* In New York City if you buy a pound of Starbucks coffee, you get a free cup of coffee. You save money on refills in all Starbucks.

* Most hotels will bring you white terrycloth bathrobes if you call housekeeping and ask for them.

* There are usually inexpensive buses or shuttles from hotels to local sightseeing spots. Inquire and be pleasantly surprised.

* Some hotels provide free transportation to and from the airport.

* Ask the front desk clerk at a hotel if you could have some extra packages of coffee for the coffeemaker in your room.

* Many hotels offer a free breakfast to enjoy before you head out to your meeting or sightseeing.

* Wait a few months and buy clothes off season when they are on sale.

* Use your airline miles for upgrades and hotel reservations.

* Use your railroad miles for free trips.

* Order an appetizer as your entrée; appetizers are usually half the price of an entrée and, besides, the smaller portion is good for your waistline.

 ＊ Discover generic brands of household products that are substantially
 lower in price than the brand-name versions.

Cheap thrills are available for the asking. You're not being cheap to
use a postcard provided by the hotel or a restaurant to write a friend.
You're doing advertising for them. Do you take the extra bar of travel
soap or shampoo home at the end of your hotel stay? Why not! You've
paid for it. Look for value added. Enjoy it. I'm well aware there is no free
lunch, but getting the most pleasure and value from our experiences and
expenditures makes perfect sense. Embrace the thrill of cheap thrills.

Take a night flight home.

BROOKE STODDARD

You Own Your Self

"Finding Oneself" is a misconception. A self is not discovered but formed by deliberate contemplation and action.

JACQUES BARZUN

Be proud to be yourself, quirks and all. Peter and I had a minister in New York City who told his parishioners to love and accept themselves, warts and all. We are unique in every definition of the word. There is just no one like us in the world; there never has been and there never will be. Even though many of our cells are renewed regularly in our bodies, we have our own DNA, our own identity, which remains the same throughout the course of our lifetime. Our essence remains constant no matter what environment we're in. What are some of your idiosyncrasies? How would you describe your one-of-a-kind characteristics? Perhaps you are loving, generous, thoughtful, kind, and compassionate. What is your most fundamental self? What are some of the small epiphanies you've experienced that have given you greater clarity and made you think, "Ah, this is me. This is who I am. This what *I* choose to do and how *I* choose to live my life"?

You never find yourself by wandering from place to place, person to person, activity to activity. You discover your true identity by what you think and what you do. Are you living the life you believe is the best one according to your essence? Are you true to your core values and beliefs, satisfying your deepest desires and wishes?

When we are true to our self, we shine most brilliantly. This is the self we should nurture, support, and encourage. Our body is the wrapping on the gift of who we are. Our environment, our looks, our possessions, are all mere trappings. You have to be *you*—in your skin, in your house, and in your activities.

The process of growing into ourselves is often painful because it requires a great deal of self-reflection and acceptance of who we really are. What can we change to improve our self? What do we have to do to become fully responsible for our lives? We have to figure it out. What "it" is, is the vital question many people never dare to face. I've never known a human being who has everything perfectly figured out, but passionately pursuing this goal yields tremendous satisfaction. Our primary task in life is to find inner peace, to be content, to become happier, more loving. Plato said it well: "The first and best victory is to conquer self."

No one can find our self for us, nor can we find self for someone else. Accept that you are not anyone else's savior. You can't expect someone to shape up, to become enlightened. Each of us must relax into self-knowledge that is the first step toward self-improvement.

Read the last words of saints, sages, and gurus; read the literature of geniuses. Be true to *your* self, and as Aristotle urged us, "Trust thyself" and a burden will be lifted from our souls. We form and reform our self. The work of self-ownership can be challenging. I know how complicated life becomes; how intertwined one choice is with another. But always remember, you own your self; I own myself. This self is all we can control; it is who we are and who we are becoming. We make wise choices not only not to sell our souls, but to live joyfully and abundantly.

Take ownership of you. Let the world know who you are and what you believe in. How you define your good life, your contributions to others, is deeply personal, individual and sacred.

Consider your invisible possessions. This is your true wealth. We earn these virtues through our own hard labor. By adopting them, we achieve the good life. The ancient philosophers defined virtue as moral excellence. Some invisible possessions may be:

* Character

* Honesty

* Sympathy

* Compassion

* Thoughtfulness

* Sensitivity

* Gratitude

* Appreciation

* Empathy

* Generosity

* Kindness

* Wisdom

* Cheerfulness

* Love

* Care

* Courtesy

* Open-mindedness

* Integrity

* Sincerity

* Humility

* Optimism

Be a student of the virtues. Seek opportunities to express them in daily life. There is so much in us that we alone must draw out. Figure it out and be true to who you are. Your finest blessing is to own your self.

To thine own self be true.

SHAKESPEARE

Stop Complaining

Complaining is not only hideously boring, but worse—
it only increases the pain.

PETER MEGARGEE BROWN

Have you noticed that almost all of our conversation has some edge of complaint? You're chatting away about whatever is bothering you, as you commiserate with someone else's problems. Apparently, approximately 85 percent of what we say is negative. This negative habit of attitude and mind is so deeply ingrained in some people it becomes their usual style of communication. Complaining easily becomes a habit. But when we wake up to how dangerous it is to be a chronic complainer, we should choose to try to stop this bad habit. Complaining only increases the pain.

There will always be things to complain about, but there are people who are so much worse off than we are, no matter what our problems are. As we become more skilled in training our minds, we can choose to cut down on our complaining. We do this internally, by not vocalizing a negative thought.

Last summer I was invited to a dear friend's wedding. I went to the final fitting for Kate's wedding dress with her mother, Barbara, also a dear friend. Afterward, we went to an art gallery next door and had a wonderful private tour of Roger Mühl's paintings there. To celebrate the day, we went across the street to the Carlyle Hotel for iced tea. We then met up with Kate's fiancé, her father, and Peter for an intimate pre-wedding celebration at a townhouse restaurant nearby. I was feeling blissful. The next morning as I left our apartment, I encountered a neighbor in the elevator. By way of being pleasant, I said, "I hope you're enjoying a wonderful summer." "No," she replied, "it has been dreadful and I don't want to get into it." I let her exit the elevator first. As I walked to the sunny street, my heart sank. My body felt heavy. I felt sad. It took some energy to shake this off. As miserable as this woman was, she was also extremely rude. If someone greets you in a caring, cheerful manner and you are experiencing a tragic time, rather than tell a lie, you can, at least, wish them well.

No one wants to be dragged down by people who complain. We're all trying to hold our own. When someone focuses on dissatisfaction or resentment, or has a grievance, it is unproductive and magnifies the situation. Eudora Welty, the beloved American writer from Jackson, Mississippi, wrote, "The excursion is the same when you go looking for your sorrow as when you go looking for your joy."

We'll never have a perfect life, but complaining causes anxiety, stress, and unhappiness thereby contaminating our internal harmony, sending the wrong signals to our brain and all our cells. We can accept what we cannot change. We can choose to keep our mind clear, moving our thoughts in the direction of how we can make things better.

There is a tendency among many people to "one up" the complainer. Someone complains about a sore back. "Well, I had back surgery and my back has hurt ever since." We want the one suffering to understand they aren't alone, that we've suffered more. But counter-complaining only magnifies the power of the negative event.

No one really wants to hear our litany of complaints. We all are doing the best we can to overcome our own difficulties and heal in our brokenness. Ask yourself, when you feel you can't control your thoughts and emotions and you complain, what are you seeking? Do we want someone to pity us? Why elicit pity in others when we could be admired for our courage, our determination, and our bravery?

I'm married to someone who rarely complains. Peter believes we should pause and try to figure things out before we complain. Look at a situation and try to find a solution. We can deliberately choose not to create a problem. I've learned so much from Peter, who is courageous in the way he faces life's inevitable challenges.

To help break the habit of expressing dissatisfaction with life, we can focus our attention on all that is good. Focus on abundance, not loss. If it rains, be glad you have an umbrella with you because you heard the weather forecast. When we back away from the nonproductive energy of complaining, we see how inappropriate it really is to grouse to someone—who is probably much worse off than we are—who has to listen to us.

Never complain to someone about his or her behavior. A friend of excellence, of great character, will not complain, "Why haven't you called me? Why haven't I heard from you?" Tell a friend how wonderful it is to be back in touch, how happy it makes you to be together.

Try not to say, "You never . . . ," or "You always . . ." This is hurtful. Whenever you complain to someone about themselves, you inevitably say some harmful things that you will later regret. Just as it is nearly impossible to hit the Golden Mean and be angry at just the right time, in the exact right proportion, for the right reason, at the right person, so it is with complaining. We never get it just right. To complain about the brutal heat, when you're at the water's edge, to someone in an un-air-conditioned apartment in New York is not wise. To complain about the drought in New England to someone who is homeless in New Orleans after Hurricane Katrina is insensitive.

Be grateful for all the good in your life. We can train our mind to accept what we have no power to change. We can be a good listener to a loved one who complains, without telling about our own misfortunes. We can be sympathetic without becoming sad. We can send our loving energy to all those who have a great deal to complain about who are struggling to focus on the good.

Think before you complain.

CARL BRANDT

25

Accept Responsibility

It takes a total commitment to a fully experienced life,
one in which no opportunities are left unexplored and no
potential undeveloped, to achieve excellence.

MIHALY CSIKSZENTMIHALYI

There are possibilities for us literally everywhere. Recognition of them is one thing, but then you have to accept the opportunity. This is active virtue. You have to step through the door and act. Are you ready? Do you accept the offer, the opportunity?

We invite opportunities and set the stage for action by our choices, our study, our concentration and commitment. But sometimes, no matter how prepared we are, no matter how much we want something, no matter how much we recognize that this could be our big break, we fail to accept the opportunity before us, perhaps because we're afraid of rejection or failure.

As actors know, you cannot get the part if you never audition. For years I wrote in spiral notebooks, longing for the opportunity to have an editor discover my potential. One evening, as I was dancing at a poolside party at a tennis club in Connecticut, a senior editor from *Reader's Digest*, Robert O'Brien, a tennis acquaintance, cut in to dance with me. We discussed my interest in being a writer and someday being published. "If there is ever anything I can do to help you as a writer," he said to me, "please let me know." Several years later, Bob O'Brien became my editor at *Reader's Digest* and excerpted a chapter from my first book.

One of the saddest thoughts is to never have discovered an enchanted garden because you never tried to reach the entrance to open the door. It is sad to think what might have been. We must always open doors knowing that there will be great possibilities awaiting us when we do. All experiences deeply lived, no matter how much we struggle, are opportunities to learn. The greatest loss occurs when we don't expose ourselves to opportunities because we may be afraid of failure. Somehow we find inner strength when we persevere courageously. When we don't try, or we give up too easily, we're turning our backs on the door that only we can open. I don't believe many of us really know how great we are in potential. We should expect more from ourselves. When we do, we bring out more from the vast reservoir of possibility that is in us all the time.

Our great task as human beings is to grow into fully expressing our powers and capacities. There is always so much more we can draw out of ourselves. There is a tendency among many of us to busy ourselves with "this and that," to fill our calendar with obligations, and to commit to responsibilities that are not of our choosing that make us believe something bigger, better, and more extraordinary is not possible.

Leave time each day to do what *you* want to do to prepare yourself for great opportunities. Grab the golden ring. Don't hold back, reticent, waiting for extraordinary opportunities. Watch for the little opportunities right now at hand. You're at a reception and meet someone who tells you of a job opening in your field. You go for an interview but are not chosen for the position. But the company recruiter and you got along well and he assured you he will keep you in mind for openings in the future. Or you read in the local newspaper about a writing contest with a cash prize. You submit an essay and cross your fingers. Two weeks later you receive a letter congratulating you for your touching piece on your grandmother, along with a check for five hundred dollars, a real windfall. Even if you didn't win, writing the article at least gave you the possibility of being published.

You will face disappointments and failures, but you can always be proud that you accepted an opportunity. Take whatever comes to you and make the best, the most good of it. You are accepting the challenge to be all you can be. Whenever we do every task the best we can, we generate more receptivity to opportunities and discover new talents and interests that give us pleasure; we learn, in time, to do more with ease. Reaching out and accepting opportunities is what we're meant to do in order to live well.

Most women are overscheduled. When you invite a friend to come for supper, if you are asked, "What can I bring?" be specific—dessert or a salad. When that door opens, don't say, "Nothing." You may need and want help. Someone asks, "What can I do for you?" Perhaps you might want someone to watch the children while you go to the post office. Accept these breaks. We can't live without help from others. When someone I love genuinely asks me what he or she can do for me, I'm more inclined to tell them now than I was when I was younger and less secure.

Actively pursue what you desire. Look for an opening, a good possibility for success. Make your own circumstances. Find the pleasure and fun where you can. Give life your all. Open gates and doors. Walk down the passageway. See the garden, experience and smell the roses. You can't imagine all the opportunities that are possible for you. We only use a small part of our powers. We're capable of becoming far more. Eleanor Roosevelt believed, "If you prepare yourself . . . you will be able to grasp opportunity for broader experience when it appears."

Accept the gift of opportunity when you find it because opportunities are fleeting and life is short.

> To improve the golden moment of opportunity and catch the
> good that is within our reach, is the great art of this life.

SAMUEL JOHNSON

Be Aware

The ultimate value of life depends upon awareness and the power of contemplation rather than upon mere survival.

ARISTOTLE

How many of us can truthfully say that we are centered in the present, mindful of what is real? How watchful and alert are we? When we are aware, we have full consciousness of something; we're mentally awake and alert. In this ideal state of consciousness and contemplation, we make appropriate, wise choices. We're quicker to recognize reality and respond in a useful, thoughtful way.

We've been given the gift of self-responsibility. The more aware we are, the more chances we'll have to use our responsibility intelligently. Through this discipline of self-discovery through ever-increasing awareness, we can think new thoughts that can make a huge difference to us and the rest of the world. William James, the nineteenth-century thinker and father of psychology, said, "A great many people think they are thinking when they are only rearranging their prejudices." He believed we are only half awake compared to what we ought to be. Being not too bad is not being good.

How aware do you feel you are of someone else's feelings? Are you generally good at reading people's body language? Can you usually tell how people feel by sensing their energy and by looking at their face, into their eyes? It is beautiful to have eye contact with someone you love and experience the softness and kindness in their eyes. How insightful and discerning do you believe you are?

How aware are you of what's going on around you and inside you? How susceptible are you to the attitudes, feelings, and circumstances of others? Do you feel you are using all your sense perceptions as well as you can? Do you feel confident about your intellectual powers? Are you able to think for yourself? Do you generally show good judgment? Do you usually make sensible choices? How good is your memory? How often do you contemplate a deeper level of existence?

Awareness is rare. How many people do you know who are truly awakened, who are able to think and do what is right, who regularly work on purifying their minds? Few of us perceive reality. We tend to color the truth in order to feel better about ourselves or to justify our behavior. Bishop Fulton Sheen once told the congregation at the Episcopal Church Saint Bartholomew in Manhattan, "Each of us makes his own weather, determines the color of the skies in the emotional universe which he inhabits." We can create our own reality by having our thought patterns correspond to our desires for the good life. We have to keep watch, be mindful, and stay present to our motivations. Are they pure?

We should be more aware of what is happening to our planet. Are we aware of the cause and effects of global warming? Our earth is in great conflict. We are in danger. Terrorism, extremism, violence, and suicide bombings preach a culture of death, not life; hate, not love; war, not peace. This is our world, this is our life, this is our situation. What are we doing to help? What are we doing to make a difference? We're all in this life together. We can no longer afford to remain limited in narrow views. We are a global society. We have to be more tolerant when we listen to other people's opinions and beliefs.

With an open, loving heart, we can listen to others without judging. Who knows when we may learn something profound? Through the world's great diversity we are given the opportunity to contemplate a broader point of view: "How boundless and free is the sky of Awareness!" the Buddha teaches us.

There is always a bigger picture than we are aware of. We never see the complete picture, though through thoughtful contemplation of the ultimate mysteries, we experience a more spacious awareness. We become more aware of complexity as well as possibilities and solutions to difficult problems. In these fleeting moments of clarity, we get out of our own way, we stop thinking what we already know, and we leap into the silent mind of the unknown. When we do grasp wisdom, even only in flashes of insight, we know a more limitless sense of our true self.

How can we sustain our wisdom? How can we keep our hearts open? How can we contemplate life from the illumination of this expanded consciousness? Although we may have lofty goals for global reform, there are basic, practical things we can do at home. We can make modest donations to causes we believe in, local and global. We can be more conscious about the way we recycle. We can pay attention to the chemicals we expose ourselves and our children to. We can try to eat more organically grown food to maintain good health. We can try to use fewer aerosols. We can use less electricity and more solar heat. By being aware, we will be making a difference. The architect and industrial designer William McDonough believes we should "reduce, reuse and recycle." We can march or bicycle to raise money for cancer and to diminish poverty and suffering around the world.

Our lives depend on our becoming more aware.

How bright the full moon of wisdom! Truly, is anything missing now?
Nirvana is right here, before our eyes.

THE BUDDHA

Your Choices Count Most in a Crisis

> Great emergencies and crises show us how much greater
> our vital resources are than we had supposed.
>
> **WILLIAM JAMES**

Nothing tries the soul more than your own personal crisis. Yet, paradoxically, opportunity comes to us in times of chaos and crisis. How we react and the difficult choices we make will cause the situation either to improve or deteriorate. These decisive situations are emotionally stressful for all concerned and often cause us to take actions that can be helpful or prove to be unhelpful. I don't know anyone who hasn't had to face many critical moments in their lives. The reality is we all will face numerous crises in the future. My heart goes out to the person facing the predicament of having to make these painful choices. Some of the people involved, perhaps paralyzed by the trauma, choose to do nothing. In most cases doing nothing is dangerous and could be irresponsible. Some of these emergency situations happen directly to us, while others take place in the lives of our family and loved ones. There is a circle of involvement in all crises. Think of some of the examples of crisis you've had to face in your own life. Perhaps a beloved relative has gotten a devastating diagnosis. Perhaps you've had to hire a lawyer to defend your interests from greedy family members. Perhaps your stepfather drives while drinking, or your mother is losing her mind.

Many of us are familiar with the unbearably tough choices that surround serious illness. When problems surface, we have to decide on one course of action or another. We must choose whether to wait and see, or to have surgery. When we're confronting a crisis, we must call upon our high skills of choice and evaluation. We are in charge of the way we handle a crisis.

When faced with a crisis, focus. Use all your powers to intelligently confront what's going on. Try to remain calm no matter how upset you feel. To do otherwise interferes with your judgment, not to mention taking a toll on your personal health and well-being. Seek the best advice available from as many professionals as you consider necessary to help you with your choices. Sometimes you will have to make rapid-fire decisions. Choose 911 when appropriate. In a true crisis there is no time to be indecisive. Make the best choice available to you.

We experience mini-crises—we don't have our photo-ID in order to board a train, our wallet has been stolen, our house has been robbed, our jewelry stolen, we break a leg, or we get shingles. It's hard to keep anything in perspective when we're faced with a mini-crisis. We tend to panic and may go into shock. But whatever happens, concentrate on "this too shall pass." These circumstances can usually be overcome.

People have a tendency not to make choices in a crisis. They become frozen. It's hard to face reality. Other people pressure us to make choices that aren't appropriate. It's hard to stay true to yourself. It's easy to panic and make snap decisions or to disagree and, in defending your position, become unglued and frustrated. Try to take the high road. It is easier said than done. But when you're in the storm, be as true to *you* as you can. Situations pass and you are going to grow through your difficulty, learning how vital your inner resources are, how you can keep your love for life even in these dark times of crisis. It's hard to believe it at the time of crisis, but you will become stronger, more compassionate, and more understanding, having faced a crisis competently. The discipline of your strong resolve to make wise choices in a crisis will lead you further on your path toward the good life.

The difficulty in life is the choice.

GEORGE MOORE

Faster Isn't Better

Even under the most favorable conditions, the present ways of life do not necessarily result in better health and greater happiness—let alone provide the proper setting for civility. Something has gone wrong with technological civilization during the past hundred years.

RENÉ DUBOS

I believe something has gone wrong. We have excessive confidence in technology. We pay a price for progress. Look around. People seem out of control in many ways. Rather than choosing to use technology and modern scientific advantages to make our lives more civilized and beautiful, some people appear to have gone too far in the opposite direction, letting their lives become dominated by the constant demands of cell phones, e-mail, and instant messaging. In order to maintain a healthy balance in my life, I've chosen to have other people help me to use technology wisely. I'm still able to write my books and do my correspondence with a fountain pen because my friend and assistant handles all the computer work for my books and checks all the e-mails from my Web site. If something needs immediate attention, Sharon answers right away. I read through all the e-mails eventually and answer some, but not all.

I see the great benefits of e-mail. I think it is wonderful, and for many businesses, a modern necessity. But we shouldn't feel bogged down by it if we choose to take a break. Are people really happier if they are caught up on reading all their e-mails? It's never-ending. They just keep coming.

Can you take a mini-vacation from today's rapid-fire communications without feeling stress?

Fast, rapid, swift, quick, hasty, active. It's all so breathtakingly exhausting. If I chose to use a computer to write a book, it would be a dreary process. I love my writing desk, gazing up at flowers, having bright sunlight splashing down on smooth white paper. I enjoy looking up words in a big dictionary, and I also like to have an encyclopedia next to me. I savor the sound of a favorite pen squeaking across the page. I can look up and contemplate. For me, writing longhand is a pathway to graceful living and more deliberate thinking. What would you change about your relationship to technology to encourage your inner peace and wise thinking?

When we value "faster" over the enjoyment of the process, we are fast-forwarding our lives and getting out of sync with the richness of the moment. We can't fully take in the scenery when we're looking at a computer screen. What's the rush? Where are you going? There is not here. Doing is not being. High gear, high speed, diminishes our appreciation of all our senses. When we can't savor sensuous pleasures, we feel unsatisfied, restless, and anxious. Many people have lost their ability to relax. A brilliant businessman keeps making one more deal after another until he stops seeing his lover, stops going on vacations, and loses his spiritual center of gravity. When we're always up doing, coming and going, we give up so much that will never come back to us. Not only do we risk snuffing out our sensuousness, we also become machine-like, go on automatic pilot. Our soul is not engaged when we're moving too fast.

When we slow down and deliberately choose to savor whatever we are doing, we can smile at our wonder, at what we're experiencing. We give ourselves ample time and space to think, to ponder, to dream, to become conscious of all our thoughts.

My favorite sixteenth-century essayist Montaigne gives an example of enjoying the pleasure in our midst: "When I dance, I dance; when I sleep,

I sleep; yes, and when I walk alone in a beautiful orchard, if my thoughts drift to far-off matters for some part of the time, for some other part, I lead them back again to the walk, the orchard, to the sweetness of this solitude, to myself."

We all get caught up in rushing. But when we can recognize this and stop for a moment, realizing that we are not enjoying what we're doing, we can take some deep breaths and bring our attention back into feeling pleasure in the present. When we slow down, we learn to become patient again. We won't interrupt people as much. We can listen to the silences. We can give someone else our undivided attention. Every day that I worked in an office at Mrs. Brown's decorating firm, I would leave for a pleasant walk at lunchtime in order to be in the natural light and soak in some natural beauty. Mrs. Brown wouldn't allow us to eat lunch at our desk. She thought it wasn't healthy to eat a meal in a business atmosphere with constant interruptions.

We should all try not to eat too fast. It takes twenty minutes for the brain to register whether we have eaten enough food and are satisfied. If we rush, we won't value the delightfully sensuous experience of eating a beautifully served, home-cooked meal with fresh ingredients.

Rather than being expedient, we should be more interested in the quality of the journey, the subtle beauty of the experience. Daniel Goleman wrote in *Emotional Intelligence,* "Life need not be regarded as an emergency about to happen." The efficient way is not always the best way. The scenic route may be most appropriate.

We are faster but not necessarily wiser or happier than people one hundred or two hundred years ago. The soul, our immaterial essence, grows when we do less with a greater sense of appreciation, a gentler manner, and a sweeter disposition. When we smile as we go through our day, we see the value of slowing down, savoring the poetry of life. We make time to enjoy the richness of fine prose, reading to a child, and when we hear, "Again, Mommy, again," we read the story again, and sometimes, again. We should readjust our priorities to be proud not of how much we get done, but of what we're able to achieve with a sense of enjoyment.

The right choices for a better, more satisfying life will favor the sensuous, beautiful experiences without rushing. We know this to be true; we must continuously remind ourselves of it in order to live the good life fully and well.

There's more to life than speeding it up.

GANDHI

Reach Out—Literally

Do not be too timid and squeamish about your actions.
All life is an experiment.

EMERSON

When I was five, my family moved from Weston, Massachusetts, to Westport, Connecticut. In the two houses where we lived in that town, my parents had to establish a rule: I could hug everyone who came in the front door, but at the back door it was a handshake! Apparently, I was a hugger with little discrimination.

Not everyone likes to reach out and hug someone, but many people do, and it isn't just human beings that thrive with touch. Rabbits thrive when taken out of their cages and petted when they are given food. When scientists discovered this, they did the same thing with premature babies. For ten minutes, three times a day, nurses would take the preemies out of their incubators and hold and stroke them. The astonishing results in this particular study were 49 percent weight gain and the babies were able to leave the hospital sooner, saving the hospital approximately five thousand dollars per child.

Love. Reach out. Touching another human being can be a powerful experience. At Unity service at Lincoln Center with Eric Butterworth, we would close the service by all joining hands and singing, "Let there be peace on earth and let it begin with me." At the end we would lift our arms up in a triumphant gesture. This created a powerful sense of unity.

Years ago, when the Episcopalian service had us stand and reach out a hand to a fellow parishioner, saying "Peace," many people felt awkward at first. The minister would come down the aisle giving everyone in reach a bear hug. Many people don't have enough love and touching. If you go to a doctor, he or she will gently touch you. Some people immediately feel better when touched in this way, almost as though the touch itself has a healing quality.

At the Heart of Happiness Conference at the Omega Institute in Rhinebeck, New York, a few years ago, there was a great jolly man who led us in chants. He actually put some of my words into song at the end of my three-hour talk on stage. He and I joined hands; everyone stood, held hands, and sang. This amazing event lasted a long, magical time. People swayed from side to side. It was joyous. The rest of the conference maintained this wonderful sense of what happiness is—letting life unfold spontaneously, letting life happen. This experience changed me. Often I ask an audience to please stand and join hands. I say a few affirming words and then we all say them together. Most people love it, but some don't.

I remember going to San Francisco to give a talk at an antiques show shortly after the ecstatic Omega experience. The talk was geared to the serious collectors who came from all over to select priceless objects. I wanted to make a warmer connection than I felt in the audience. It was a totally unplanned moment. The spirit moved me to ask everyone to all stand: "Please hold hands." Everyone did. I asked the audience to repeat after me: "Let there be happiness in my soul and let it begin with me." As I left the tent, people came up to me and hugged me, thanking me. My dear friend who has been running the show since its inception twenty-five years ago laughed at me and with me. "Sandie, this isn't church." "It is now," I said. We had a good giggle.

At a library event recently, when I asked everyone to join hands, the bookseller, who was behind a big table stacked with books to be signed, bounded down to join the group. Again, it was magical. We all experienced a sense of connection and love. These moments can't be forced, but when they happen, we feel happy. We thrive.

Reach out to others, literally. Experience the joyful energy. Give a "high five." It makes two people feel terrific. Get on your knees, outstretch your arms to a young child, and watch and feel the love unfold in your arms.

> It is common sense to take a method and try it. If it fails,
> admit it frankly and try another. But above all, try something.

FRANKLIN DELANO ROOSEVELT

Privacy Please

For without the private world of retreat, one becomes
virtually an unbalanced creature.

ELEANOR MCMILLEN BROWN

Having a private room intended for our exclusive use is a privilege. My Zen writing room at the cottage is always there waiting for me. Everything in this modest-sized space is mine. I have my books, boxes of memorabilia, and notebooks. It's all set up, ready for me to be alone. This is my own private space.

Even if we don't have a room of our own, there are times when we'll want and need privacy and can close the door. We all need times to be secluded from sight to maintain our balance, safe from the intrusions of others. When I'm in a hotel room and put the plastic tag on the door—PRIVACY PLEASE—I feel safe and relaxed knowing that I won't be intruded upon. We all need times when we're not available.

Two summers ago I was in serious need of time alone. We were having a wedding at our home in a few weeks. We couldn't use the garden during that week because the house was being painted, so this was a rare, quiet moment's peace. I chose to put on sunscreen and escape to the Zen garden at the far end of our backyard, where I sat in my sleeveless nightgown in the sun. Pen in hand, I looked around, savoring the peace before I began to write. Suddenly I heard a noise: "Hello? Hello?" I didn't have a moment to cover up before a woman appeared. She'd apparently knocked on the front door and when there was no answer, she walked around to the back gate and felt comfortable walking through.

Peter was at the table under the umbrella reading the newspaper. This woman walked right by Peter and came up to me. I did not know this person. It was clearly not a convenient time for me. I was hiding from the world in the privacy of my own backyard. This was not an appropriate visit. The back gate is not to be opened by anyone without invitation. It's closed for privacy. I remember saying, "I'm sorry, another time."

I try to be generous with my time. I love my readers and feel blessed that many people feel a close connection to me, but I can't be randomly interrupted and lose my sense of concentration and my time for privacy. There have to be times when we're not available, not approachable, and we should try to be sensitive to other people's needs and desire for privacy.

The writer, teacher, and philosopher Joseph Campbell said this of privacy: "Sacred space and sacred time and something joyous to do is all we need. Almost anything then becomes a continuous and interesting joy."

We all do our best thinking when we are alone and quiet. Are there places or special spaces in your life where you can have sacred time alone? Is the radio turned off? If you're with a loved one, do you respect the silence and not talk on the telephone? Peter and I enjoy solitude for two. Do you spend your sacred time in a room at a pretty desk or in a cozy armchair, or do you take a quiet walk? Often, when I want a few moments of blissful solitude without interruptions, I do some ironing. My ironing board is one of my meditation spots that is always private.

When we're private, we're free to be silent in order to read, write, dream, think, and muse without talking or interruptions. This quiet time is sacred, soulful, and sweet. We come away renewed and transformed. This self-recharging should take place daily, even if only for minutes here and there. This private experience is all about you, when you fill up your own well. It is not about society, but solitude. One of my favorite books of Emerson's is his gem *Society and Solitude*. In his essay, "Work and Days," he muses:

* "But life is good only when it is magical and musical, a perfect timing and consent . . . "

* "We must be at the top of our condition to understand."

* "There can be no greatness without abandonment."

* "A song is no song unless the circumstances are free and fine."

Our privacy should be respected. One of the great punishments of a hospital or prison is lack of privacy. We need to be able to be alone to enjoy a secluded walk in the woods. Every day I make a point of going for a walk alone. If you have a dog to walk, you are blessed. You can enjoy solitude for two. Practice sitting in a room quietly and let the silence speak to you. Try to do this every day without interruption.

Our artist friend Roger Mühl's wife fiercely protects his privacy. They live in a village in Provence and everyone respects his need to walk about and be silent. He's inspired by his environment and enjoys being with friends but only when the timing is right and doesn't interfere with his work. Everyone who is trying to create something, to bring it forth, needs to be alone. Poets express this need best. In the words of the romantic poet William Wordsworth: "When from our better selves we have too long been parted by the hurrying world, and droop, sick of its business, of its pleasures tired, how gracious, how benign, is solitude." When we recognize and honor this basic need for privacy for ourselves, we live a richer, fuller, deeper, better life.

The happiest of all lives is a busy solitude.

VOLTAIRE

A Free Day for You

"I did nothing today." "What? Did you not live? That is not only the
most fundamental but the most illustrious of your occupations."

MONTAIGNE

ake in a deep breath. What might a free day feel like to you? When
was the last time you had a free day? There are so many serendipitous
fortunate discoveries we come upon spontaneously when we have an
empty day. Free from restraints, we're blessed with white spaces in our
calendar. We awaken to no appointments. We're at liberty, not controlled
by obligations or the will of others. We're free to come and go, to love life
on our own terms, to set ourself free. We have discretionary time. We're
not burdened or trapped. We're able to exercise our judgment. It's up to
us to decide how to fill our days enjoyably and wisely.

On a free day, let your experience evolve. Have an open heart. You can
choose to do one thing and then switch gears and do something else. This
sense of free choice is extremely healthy for us. Whenever we give the
spirit freedom, we are moved to do whatever seems most appealing at the
moment. No dates. No obligations. No e-mail. No fax machine. There
is nothing you have to do or should do. You are taking a break in order
to rejuvenate, revive, renew, and restore your spirit. It does wonders for
us to remove ourselves from our usual work and from being in charge of
caring for the children.

Imagine that you are able to take a day off from everything and
everyone. What do you think you'd be inclined to do? Sleep late? Get up
early? Where would you go? Would you stay home and paint the picket

fence? Would you go fishing alone or would you choose to bring your son or daughter with you? Would you go sailing? Alone? Would you play golf? Would you work in the garden and then get a cool refreshing glass of iced tea and read a good book in the hammock until you fell asleep to the sounds of the birds?

By turning our backs on our purposefulness, on our regular activities, we open up to the flow of silent mind that is inside us. What is it that's been missing in our busy, fast-paced life of pressures, schedules, and deadlines? We all need to take a break in order to recharge ourselves.

Give yourself this gift of a free day. Claim a personal day for you. This is a day you are not on call. No meetings, no conference calls, no meals to prepare for the family, no expectations from others of what you ought to do or should do. All the things you wish to do and don't get to, you're now free to begin. Open the windows and doors to your soul. Let the light spill in. If you can't spend your life exactly the way you'd choose to, for whatever reasons, you can choose to have a free day you call your own. Break away from your daily details and routines. Relax into this spacious experience. You may prefer to improve your mind by reading and listening to tapes about history and philosophy. Many professionals lament that they only have time to read about their special field and never feel caught up. A whole day of studying great literature could be a real tonic to jump-start this as a daily discipline in the future.

When we fully accept this free day, we will reconnect to our passions and bring this spaciousness with us when we return to our normal pattern of living. Some people can't even envision what it would feel like to experience this sense of freedom because they have so many real burdens in their lives. But I'm a great believer in taking whatever steps are possible to live a good life that is pleasant. A free day might be a real necessity in order for you not to lose sight of who you are, the "me" of you. When you're completely in charge of your choices, even if for just a day, you will discover more about your own needs that have to be satisfied. The more you care for the needs of others, the more you have to give yourself time for personal development. Give yourself this day to put your life in better perspective. See how everything appears to be less overwhelming, less stressful.

After you have fully lived a free day for *you,* review what you learn about your *self,* not in relationship to others, but your core identity. What did you choose to do for you? Who did you choose to be with? Who did you choose not to be with? What were the most wonderful discoveries you made about you?

Maybe you chose to have a three-hour lunch with a friend at a restaurant and then go to a museum because when you stay at home you are tempted to do chores. Or you might have chosen to swim and play tennis and go to a concert with your spouse, whom you invited to join you on your free day. You realized how long it had been since you both were free, together, without the children. You wanted to be carefree again, the way you were before you became parents.

Whatever you choose, have a rich, wonderful day. This is for you, and only you choose what you do, when you do it, where, and with whom. Why you spent your free day the way you did will be revealed to you. This free day can be pure bliss. This is my wish for you.

Give me books, fruit, French wine and fine weather and a
little music out of doors, played by someone I do not know.

JOHN KEATS

Good Design Matters

If something is good once, it's always good . . .
Mother Nature is always the best designer.

VAN DAY TRUEX

I've never been interested in fads or trends because they don't last. I believe we should trust the logic of our eye, educate our eye by exposing ourselves to as much beauty as possible, and select the best, safest, most functional, most beautiful designs available.

Just as we should be graceful in our movement, so the inanimate objects we live with can be graceful and beautiful as well. I am true to my passion for nature in the designs I'm drawn to, because they echo what we see in our natural environment. Be it a wood mantel that is hand carved with garlands of flowers or a collection of seashells from the beach, I love to see nature introduced in the objects around me.

My training as an interior designer was to use the eighteenth century as the model of man-made excellence in proportion, scale, quality, and beauty in furniture. Before machines mass-produced turned legs on chairs and tables, they were hand carved by an artisan who tenderly brought out the inner beauty of the natural material.

Nonetheless, a great deal of good design is available today that is simplified and mass made at reasonable prices. It shows influences from the past, but there is a newness, a refreshing simplicity that is appealing. We build on what is ideal. By looking at the real thing, at the best examples of good design, we're able to select more affordable objects that are pretty, have grace and charm, and are pleasing to our senses, as well as practical for the way we live today.

As you know, there is a great deal of ugly, bad design available from all corners of the world. The good is right next to the horrible. Reject at least 90 percent of everything you see because it is not beautiful. Beauty is always the guiding principle of good design. Good design, and good taste, give pleasure and have great influence on our lives.

Only your eye and your heart know what will make you happy. Nothing could be more personal. In 1959 in Hong Kong, I had an emerald-green brocade dress made. It had a mandarin collar and sexy high slits on either side of a long straight-cut skirt. I completely identified with this dress. I felt radiant when I wore it. All these years later, I find I'm drawn to wearing clothes with mandarin collars made in China. This style is classic. We can find good design everywhere when we're discerning and patient. Good design can be strikingly plain because when the scale, proportion, shape, and colors are attractive, the object is appealing.

I love to use my favorite serrated tomato knife with its blue-and-white striped handle to cut up fruit and vegetables. I've learned that these colors and the stripes give me a real lift. I have several knives with black handles that stay unused in the drawer because this one inexpensive knife helps me do what is necessary with ease, pleasure, and fun. Good practical design can turn a chore into a ritual.

Purposefully choose well-designed, functional objects. Poorly designed, ugly objects that don't function frustrate us and cause unnecessary accidents, blocking our energy. If the olive oil container drips, what could have been a pleasant dinner becomes an icky mess. If the coffee carafe sloshes when poured, a simple refill becomes a cleanup of stained clothing, table, or chair. These things matter.

I am drawn to hand-blown glasses. I bought a pretty, square, clear glass with a yellow rim. The first time I sipped from it, water dripped all over my blouse. Lucky it wasn't red wine. I now use this pretty glass as a flower vase.

Good design should be safe as well as functional. Imagine what happens in houses in a flood zone that don't even give people access to their own roofs. A coffee table with a floating edge could poke a child's eye out or badly gash someone's knee. A three-legged stool is not safe to sit on. A three-legged table flips over if someone leans on it, spilling everything.

Good, responsible, attractive design can make a huge difference in our lives. If the clippers you use to prune and cut your flowers are well designed for easy and efficient use, their functional beauty will make your time spent with your flowers a lot more enjoyable. A can opener or peppermill can be attractive and do the job well. A wine opener that works reliably makes the celebration more enjoyable.

Whether you select a wine glass, flatware, flower vase, pair of shoes, scarf, sofa, storage unit, tablecloth, pajamas, or set of sheets, these objects are instruments that make up your whole symphony. Strive to choose good design in all the aspects of your life. Good design creates a warm, comfortable atmosphere and feeling of beauty at home or wherever we are.

Nothing need ever be ugly or badly designed. We can—and should—
be surrounded by beautiful things all through our day-to-day lives.

WALTER HOVING

Enough Is Enough

You never know what is enough unless you know
what is more than enough.

WILLIAM BLAKE

The good life is a happy life, and our happiness helps to promote happiness in others. Doing only what is good for us, without considering the common good, could lead to greed, insensitivity, and excess. Excess is always bad. The good life is a life of active virtue, of real personal excellence, where the choices we make are not only good for us but also enhance other people's sense of pleasure and well-being.

In your choices, try to aim for the moderate position that is reasonable and compassionate both toward others and yourself. Any action we take should be one that is good—good for us, for the nourishing of our inner life and our soul, and good for our extended family, our neighbors, our business relationships, our community, and our planet home. The real excellence of the good life is found in the center, not in the extremes of too much or too little. Here, all of our needs are met, as well as our desires that are good for us.

Over the past several years, as I've studied the principal elements that make for a good life, I've tried to be a keen observer of people's behavior. I've read and heard about brazen, flagrant, insolent acts of excess. Many people are out of control. Enough to many is clearly not enough. They've reached the point where any potential good becomes bad—dangerous, dishonest, or greedy to the point of decadence. Some people have lost all caring and sensitivity to the needs and desires of others. I call this "extreme excess syndrome," or "EE." We must recognize and reject this excessive behavior. I believe we should take a stand and not hesitate to express our feelings in a nice way whenever we feel it is appropriate.

Recently I was on a train, seated in the café car where I was able to spread out my work on a table. This car has the best air-conditioning on the train, as well as having great light because of the large picture windows. Peter and I are regulars on this train. However, on this particular trip, for three hours a contractor tried to conduct his business on his cell phone in zones where he had bad connections. "Can you hear me?" he'd scream. I whispered, "We can all hear you so loudly you thunder inside our brain." He'd eat and talk and become so frustrated he'd slam the phone down and swear. He was too thoughtless and too lazy to go sit in the phone booth at the end of the car. He was in out-of-service zones, but he kept screaming and banging and swearing. This man was bursting his gut, infuriated. You could see veins protruding on his temples. He could have had a heart attack or a stroke. His behavior was not good for him, and it wasn't good for the rest of us, either. The conductor finally made an announcement—in an attempt to have this man be more considerate—but the contractor was too upset to listen. The train was crowded. I chose to stay where I was because otherwise I'd have to waste these precious hours in a car that was too dark for reading or writing. I realize when I'm on public transportation I'm at the mercy of fellow passengers. It's not the same as home where Peter and I leave the room to talk on the telephone in order not to disturb the concentration of the other, who is working at the desk.

Some people's work is quiet and doesn't disturb people around them. I've noticed that the cell phone has taken people out of their office and they do their business now at restaurants, bars, outdoor cafés, and on trains and planes. No matter how beautiful a place is where you go to enjoy a pleasurable experience, the cell phones surround you, invading your inner peace and diluting the sensuous experience. EE. Wonderful new science, carried to extremes. If two people are at a restaurant together and one person is on his cell phone, the other person eats alone and sits there, ignored. EE.

Another excess is television viewing. This technology was going to bring us such happiness. The world would come into our family room. George Gerbner, a researcher who studied violence on television, identified a "mean world syndrome," a phenomenon in which people who watch large amounts of television are more likely to believe that the world is an unforgiving and frightening place. What has happened is EE, where people, on average, watch twenty-four hours of television a week. It's mindless. You sit there passively, allowing the brain to stagnate. Everything is done for you. The brain needs to be used or we lose it. Not only does excessive television viewing restrict proper stimulation of the brain and expose us to violence, but studies show that television advertising has a negative impact on one's happiness because it makes us feel we need things we previously didn't need or want.

The overall effect of television in programming as well as advertising is to make us want more. The great paradox is that this wonder box actually creates discontent: we're less happy with our bodies when skinny young models flaunt their bodies on the screen. Our spouses are less happy with us. We are less happy with our possessions. We think the Joneses are happier and wealthier, smarter, younger, and prettier than they really are. Television affects our behavior. The brilliant English economist Richard Layard wrote in an insightful book, *Happiness: Lessons from a New Science*, that for every extra hour of television we watch, we spend an extra four dollars, give or take a few cents. This is as serious as a gambling addiction when you multiply hours and dollars per week, per month, per year. EE.

Layard cites the latest scientific studies, and he believes that television increases peer pressure. Children are the most impressionable viewers of advertising who "want what their friends have, need the same things in order to keep up." He is glad that Sweden has banned commercial advertising directed at children under the age of twelve and he hopes other countries will do this also. Layard suggests we cut down on reading magazine ads and catalogues. Einstein cautioned scientists to make theories as simple as possible but not simpler. In order to avoid excess, for ourselves and our children, we have to be mindful of the difference between our needs and our desires and be sure our wants are good for us.

A study involving 16,000 people, aged 20 to 64, showed that happiness can remain elusive to people who are in never-ending competition with keeping up with the Joneses' bank account. Glenn Firebaugh, a sociologist at Pennsylvania State University, writes, "Our analysis indicates that Americans are on a hedonic treadmill for most of their working lives. We find—with and without controls for age, physical health, education and other correlates of happiness—that the higher the income of others in one's age group, the lower one's happiness." The cheerful news this study showed is that the biggest predictor of happiness was not wealth, but health, then income, education, and marital status. The greatest source of unhappiness is comparisons.

Socrates, Plato's teacher in ancient Greece, is said to have pleaded, "I have no concern at all for what most people are concerned about: financial affairs, administration of property . . . but rather the one where I could do the most good to each one of you in particular, by persuading you to be less concerned with what you *have* than with what you *are*; and that you make yourselves as excellent and as rational as possible."

Scale is key to balance. We don't value our life by what we have, but by who we are and what we are doing with our lives. Euripides, the ancient Greek dramatist, taught us, "Enough is abundance to the wise." Look at the people who have what you think you want. Do you feel these things make them happy? Do they complain about the expense and maintenance? Do they have ample time, away from the marketplace, to make themselves more excellent? Ideally, we want to have things that enhance our ability to freely do what we choose to do. When you think about *you,* contemplate who *you* are in your essential nature, not what you have. Too much money or too many possessions cloud our focus when we could be nurturing our soul. A garden creates a secret place of beauty and refuge, but it doesn't have to be large. Excess takes away our freedom and we become bogged down.

The fewer our material desires, the more freedom we have to live well, to grow in wisdom and understanding. We own our self, not what we possess. When we reduce our attachments, as the Buddha teaches us, we end our suffering. Dwell on what you have, not what you lack. Choose the best quality over the greatest quantity. Consider giving away or selling off some of your stuff. How much of it do you actually use? Less is more, as the architect Mies van der Rohe believed. Best is what is good, what is moderate, what is in the center, not the extremes.

Think of Michelangelo, who was happiest when he had a chisel in his hand. "The idea is there, locked inside, and all you have to do is remove the excess stone." Chip away, take away. As you read the newspaper ads, look for EE. Think of Shakespeare, who understood about EE: "To gild refined gold, to paint the lily, to throw a perfume on the violet, to smooth the ice, or add another hue unto the rainbow, or with taper-light to seek the beauteous eye of heaven to garnish, is wasteful and ridiculous excess."

Enough is enough. We should eat only three meals a day. Some people are excessive about possessing shoes. You'll never be poor when you know when enough is enough. By being satisfied with less, we're spiritually wealthy.

Extreme Excess syndrome is not good for our society or for us. When we accept enough is truly enough, the center will hold.

The secret of contentment is knowing how to enjoy what you have, and to be able to lose all desire for things beyond your reach.

LIN YUTANG

Give Yourself Time

Our patience will achieve more than our force.

EDMUND BURKE

Be patient with yourself and others. Patience is a virtue and should be your choice. A doctor's secret is that patients cure themselves. The main reason doctors will tell us to take it easy is that they don't want us to interfere with the natural healing that takes place in the cells and immune system of our bodies. If a doctor believes a patient is mentally stable and really wants to help in the recovery from an injury, illness, or surgery, he may prescribe "Activity as tolerated." If we overdo, we suffer and have setbacks.

We have to get off our own backs and not be unreasonably hard on ourselves. Every situation will last as long as it lasts. If you are recovering from a medical procedure, how you will bounce back is personal. A doctor can only guess based on his experience with other patients. Nature teaches us great patience because everything comes slowly in its own season. This slow process makes the rebirth of spring so exuberant, such a lift to our spirits. We have faith, understanding that in the winter the roses are dormant. When they aren't in full bloom, hugging the picket fence and perfuming the air as they do in July, I buy cut roses at the grocery store. I arrange them in vases to place around the cottage. They cheer us up and remind us of the pace of nature: after winter, spring does come.

We have to choose to be patient with ourselves when we are going through a rough patch or a time of major transition. The poet Longfellow wrote, "All things come around to him who will but wait." Don't be hard on yourself when you're making really difficult lifestyle choices and changes. It isn't easy to change our habits. Make a deliberate point not to become frustrated by the timing of the outcome. Remind yourself that you are trying hard, doing the best you can, to accept the situation you're in. In order for a new habit to become second nature, we need to consciously avoid or alter our old way of thinking and reprogram new disciplined thoughts. This takes time and patience but is well worth the effort.

We shouldn't set ourselves up for failure. Try not to set rigid deadlines for when you want something to be resolved or when you will be free of pain; this will cause unnecessary stress on your immune system. You're trying to maintain equilibrium and self-control in a tough time. Be willing to tolerate delays and setbacks. Choose not to get annoyed. When you exhibit a calm understanding while trying to grow through these difficulties, you will ease the pain. While my friend and literary agent was recovering from a leg operation last year, he ended a conversation with: "I'm learning how to walk again. This is where we are now. It's all good."

All of us have to face difficult situations at one time or another. Resign yourself to do what you can that is appropriate to your circumstances and calmly, clear mindedly work toward the outcome or result. Don't act hastily or impulsively. Wise Emerson reminds us that "Every sweet hath its sour." Even perfect roses have thorns. We have to accept the not so good in order to make the best of reality.

I don't know anyone who is on easy street. We all have sadness even when we are living a good, happy life. We choose to endure and be persevering. When you find yourself in a muddle, when you don't know what you want, when what you want isn't happening, or when you feel overwhelmed by circumstances that have caused you great misfortune, give yourself time. Things won't seem so raw; pain won't be as acute, six months or a year from now. Learning to live alone after your spouse dies takes time. Studies indicate it can take several years before husbands or wives are back to their usual set point of happiness. The powerful choice is to be patient even if the period of suffering is long. Anything that happens to us happens to others. All healing—mental, emotional, physical, and spiritual—requires time and patience; this is a true need that requires moral courage.

When you're learning something new and may not understand it right away, keep at it. Out of the blue, the brain will make the necessary connections. I read Aristotle, for instance, in the mornings when I am fresh from sleep, because, while he is brilliant, he is not easy to read. The more I study his works, however, the more I understand his practical, useful, uncommon commonsense philosophy. He teaches us that if we wish to understand things, we must watch them develop; it takes time for what we have learned to become our nature.

The genius Albert Einstein admitted, "I think and think for months, for years. Ninety-nine times the conclusion is false. The hundredth time I am right." Every morning Claude Monet would wait for the right moment for the light to come around once more. He was able to celebrate when he declared, "I have broken through the envelope, the opaque surface of things. Odd that it should have taken so long to reach this point, knowing it, as I did, to be my element."

What are some areas in your life where you feel you need to be more patient?

- Be patient when you're with people who walk slower than you do.

- When someone doesn't hear you, patiently repeat yourself.

- Make it a habit not to interrupt when people talk slowly or pause to think. When we are impatient, we feel superior, but we really lack compassion.

- Understand that nature cures us when we are recovering from an illness; we should allow the healing process to flow through us in its own time.

- Give yourself time to heal after a loss.

Trust. Wait. Hope. Believe. Love. Meditate. Patience is a sign of genius— certainly a badge of courage. We're all part of humanity. We're all in it together. We have to have the humility to give others and ourselves time.

Even a happy life cannot be without a measure of darkness, and the word "happy" would lose its meaning if it were not balanced by sadness. It is far better to take things as they come along with patience and equanimity.

CARL JUNG

Get Going

I find the great thing in this world is not so much where we stand as in what direction we are moving: To reach the port of heaven, we must sail sometimes with the wind and sometimes against it—but we must sail, and not drift, nor lie at anchor.

OLIVER WENDELL HOLMES

Vital activity propels happiness. The cure for the blues is to get going and do something that delights you. A ten-minute brisk walk produces positive feelings and increased energy for up to two hours afterward. Walking clears our head and gives us vitality.

Studies have shown that people who participate in an aerobics class two to four times a week for eight to ten weeks have an increased set point of happiness and reduced clinical depression and anxiety. Because of this exercise regime, people can do stressful tasks with less effort and negative effect on their heart rate and blood pressure.

Sports activities and exercise, as we know, release endorphins, the body chemicals that make us feel better. Social interaction with others—any leisure activity done in a group—is a source of happiness. This is particularly true for extroverts. What are some of the activities you enjoy that increase your good mood? How many things do you do regularly that are energetic activities?

Experts tell us we're supposed to take 10,000 steps a day in order to feel robust, strong, and vigorous. To some of us who spend hours sitting in a chair at a desk, this could sound exhausting. But all of us move around more than we realize, doing a variety of different things. I find that when I'm doing housework, if I put on some peppy music, I flow through necessary chores feeling energetic from the moving and doing. I try to climb stairs whenever I can.

The dance impresario Martha Graham makes us realize how important it is to express ourselves through our movements. Studies show that dancing and music greatly enhance our mood. Graham believed, "There is a vitality, a life force, an energy, a quickening, that is translated through you into action, and because there is only one of you in all time, this expression is unique. And if you block it, it will never exist through any other medium and will be lost."

Even for older people, dancing brings great joy. I love going to a resort and watching elderly couples out on the dance floor enjoying themselves. Older people can join social clubs that keep them active; they can play golf, garden, do hobbies, and make walking a regular habit. What makes it easier, more natural, for some people to get going while others tend to get stuck? What keeps us from getting a jump-start?

* We fear failure, rejection, or the unknown.
* We can't make up our mind what to do.
* We feel scattered; we can't concentrate.
* We're afraid we won't be accepted.
* We don't have confidence.
* Procrastination becomes a habit.
* We don't feel well.
* We're sad.

Research shows that the greatest satisfaction comes from activities that require a degree of challenge. When we have the skills to be able to do something well, it makes us happy. To a nongolfer, it seems silly to walk around whacking a small white ball, trying to drop it into a little hole in the ground. But I have friends who are serious golfers and they find it exhilarating to play well. When they get a hole-in-one, they feel ebullient. A birdie is exciting.

When you can't get going physically, it is wise to be cerebral by exercising your mind. Heavy television watchers are less happy than others.

When you go on a holiday, do you have a tendency to be more active then usual? In one study of people who suffer from headaches, while they were on vacation only 3 percent had headaches, compared to 21 percent when they were not on holiday. Does this indicate that when people are away from home, when they can catch up on their sleep, be free of work obligation and the pressures of a stressful lifestyle, they are more relaxed?

Participate in activities that will reap the greatest rewards. When the bathroom floor needs to be cleaned, this will be satisfying if you do it spontaneously, on the spur of the moment, not as a chore, but as a form of exercise. When you feel romantic, go dancing. When you feel like ironing, that's the time to do it.

What do you want to do? What do you believe you ought to do? Get going and do it. What direction do you want to move in, what do you want to accomplish? Take some steps as well as some risks, so you can bring out what you already have inside you.

Take action. Aristotle spoke of "active virtue." Once you know something to be true for you, you should choose to spring into action. When we're alive, we must keep moving. Try not to make too many plans, however. Overscheduling puts us in a rigid box. Far better to let the spirit move us in the direction that is most useful at the time. Whatever you choose to do, be lively and sustain enthusiasm as you energetically engage in an activity. Antoine de Saint Exupéry said, "It is in your act that you exist, not in your body. Your act is yourself, and there is no other you." Do things that stimulate your love of life. The feisty, bright, and charming actress Katharine Hepburn went for a swim every morning in the cold Connecticut River in back of her house in Fenwick. One of her favorite sayings was, "Let's do it!"

There is joy in being energetic, dynamic, and vigorous. As we all know, the more we exert ourselves physically, mentally, and spiritually, the more vigor we'll have, the more life force we have to reach our full potential. Being vital is living well. Get going. Identify your concerns, interests, and intentions. Address them. Get started. If you choose to begin an exercise regime, make an appointment in your calendar and get started. We are halfway there when we begin.

I do not know what I may appear to the world; but to myself I seem to have been only like a boy playing on the seashore, and diverting myself now and then by finding a smoother pebble or prettier shell, whilst the great ocean of truth lay all undiscovered before me.

SIR ISAAC NEWTON

Embrace Variety

Variety is the soul of pleasure.

APHRA BEHN

Just as we use only a fraction of our brain's capacity, we don't take advantage of the enormous number of choices we have in every area of our lives. In the food we eat, the clothes we wear, the colors we surround ourselves with, the objects we collect, the people we choose to be with, the intellectual activities we enjoy, and the places we want to explore in our travels, we have a tendency to limit ourselves unnecessarily.

Surveys indicate that our enjoyment of a favorite ice cream flavor diminishes if we taste it every day for a prolonged period of time. The unusual, when it becomes usual, lessens our pleasure. Studies prove that when we eat the same diet day after day, it becomes toxic and the body may be harmed as our pleasure decreases.

According to some ayurvedic practitioners, there are six different varieties of taste: sweet, sour, salty, bitter, pungent, and astringent. When we enjoy spices, our metabolism rises by an astonishing 25 percent. Approximately 80 percent of taste is linked to smell. One thing always leads to another. When we broaden our food categories to incorporate all six varieties of taste, we will also increase the variety of our sensual pleasures of taste, smell, sight, and touch.

Few pleasures last long without variety. We are stimulated to travel to a different city, to explore a museum we've never been to before, to go to a remote island on vacation, or to try out a new restaurant. Life is throbbing with excitement. It is up to us to choose to step out of our safe routines and embrace fresh opportunities everywhere, finding new interests and discovering exciting adventures.

Dr. René Dubos, the wise student of human nature, once said, "I am happy that there are on earth many worlds, instead of One World, because diversity enriches human life." Wherever we travel, we will experience a unique spirit of place. Sometimes we feel at home in a foreign country because we feel a soulful connection. While I'm as American as apple pie, I'm drawn to the energy, the beauty, the smells and light of Provence. I would be blind to all the happiness this part of France has provided for me over the past forty-five years if I hadn't saved up all my change in mayonnaise jars to go see this charming place for myself.

The more we embrace variety, the more intensely active and alive we'll become. Scientists are encouraging us to have more variety in our activities in order to keep the brain stimulated. We're encouraged to perform mental calisthenics to try to keep our minds from fading, thus reducing the risk of Alzheimer's or other dementia.

The use-it-or-lose-it theory shows strong evidence that the more intellectually stimulating our activities—learning Italian, going to lectures and the theater, reading, playing chess or bridge, or other hobbies, or learning how to play a musical instrument, the less likely we are to develop Alzheimer's. Scientists suspect that a lifetime of deep thinking may create a "cognitive reserve"—a reservoir of brainpower—we can draw upon. Just as our body stores fat, our brain stores up all of our thinking, which is there for us as a vast cerebral storeroom.

Rob Stein, writing about the mysteries of the brain for the *Washington Post,* reported that many researchers suspect "people may benefit most from engaging in a rich diversity of stimulating activities. New experiences may be far more important than repeating the same task over and over." Studies have found that combining mental stimulation with social interaction appears to be highly beneficial. "Experts say the task should be enjoyable, because stress and other negative emotions appear harmful," according to Stein's report.

Around the country, scientists have launched brain training sessions: elderly people take up quilting and acting classes, and volunteer as tutors or as librarians. "It was pretty amazing," said Michelle Carlson of Johns Hopkins in Baltimore, whose team found that the elderly volunteers scored much better on problem-solving tests than before their training and that their frontal lobes seem to have been invigorated. "We observed changes that appeared to show that their brains were functioning more like [those of] younger adults." The bottom line: cutting-edge scientific research shows that not only should we exercise our bodies regularly, but we also should regularly exercise the "muscle" called our mind. We are never too young to concern ourselves with our memories. Dr. Gary Small of UCLA is worried about our ability to maintain our mental abilities. In a certain study, participants had a brain scan before and after going through a two-week "memory prescription" program consisting of a healthful diet, regular exercise, relaxation techniques, and memory exercises. The findings were that in everyday memory, participants' brains worked more efficiently after following the program. We can all make up our own memory exercises. Try to remember one piece of a family member's wardrobe each morning, for instance. I find that once I write something down, I tend to remember it substantially better than when I don't put pen to paper.

What I find so compelling is that the bigger, richer, fuller our lives are, the more varied, diverse, and broad our interests, the more we will be reducing the harmful effects of stress and negative emotions, stimulating our brains, and becoming happier. We're built to fully experience the marvels all around us and everywhere. Wise people have been telling us for years that the good life is good for us. As my friend Mary Ellen McCarthy, who lives across the street from me in Stonington Village, loves to say, "How great is that!"

The first century B.C. Greek philosopher Publilius Syrus understood:

"No pleasure endures unseasoned by variety." How can we keep ourselves from getting into ruts? How can we add variety to our routine?

I enjoy changing the location where I routinely work. I find this stimulating. Sometimes I sit outside in our tiny garden, or I'll leave my writing table in the Zen room and go sit by a cozy fire in the living room in the winter. The kitchen table is a great comfort when I need a change. The key is not to be rigid and inflexible as you go about your regular routine. Each day, add some new experiences to your life to benefit from the stimulation of variety:

* Try a new recipe.

* Learn a new word and use it in your vocabulary.

* Browse through an encyclopedia and learn something you never knew about—perhaps Egyptian architecture or Japanese literature.

* Study up on all the different varieties of your favorite flowers.

* Taste a flavor of ice cream you've never tried.

* Learn all the different varieties of butterflies you see in your yard.

* Identify all the birds you see.

* Study some aspect of astronomy.

* Plan a trip to a country you've never been to before.

* Wear a different color combination.

* Set the table with a new fresh coordination of plates, placemats, napkins, and glasses.

* Use a different color ink in your fountain pen.

* Go to an ethnic restaurant and eat according to the custom of the culture.

* Write a poem to a friend instead of a letter.

* Expose yourself to a new and different spiritual experience, always

searching, ever deepening and strengthening your inner life through diversity.

* Go to a favorite museum and explore permanent exhibits you've never seen. Listen to the audiotape. Take notes.

* Go to an entirely different part of town to buy your groceries.

* Try a new tea or coffee flavor.

* Take all of the objects off your living room tables and surfaces. Put everything back in a new, fresh way.

* If you're right handed, do simple tasks with your left hand—this is good for the brain's balance.

* If you're accustomed to e-mailing everyone for communication, try writing short notes or postcards by hand, or use the fax or telephone.

* Rather than photographing something you find beautiful, sketch it with a pencil or pastels.

* Each year plant different color tulips or lilies.

* Move your art around to keep your eye fresh.

The more we embrace variety, the greater our chances of enjoying our lives fully right to the end.

From there to here, and here to there, funny things are everywhere.

DR. SEUSS

Move On

With no looking back at what might have been, and we are at peace.

ROSE FITZGERALD KENNEDY

We live our lives in chapters. We have to learn to let go of what's over or we will suffer. We know attachments cause suffering. The Buddha urged us to learn to let go. From my extensive research on happiness, I've learned that study after study indicates that dwelling on what was once wonderful or awful can dampen our spirits for the present.

The most intelligent way to move in the direction of a good life is to live each day, each experience, as authentically as we can, with integrity, honesty, and courage. Life today, it appears, is becoming more complex, not less so. No matter how committed we are to finding pleasure in the journey of the moment, many of us feel so much stress that we merely want to get through situations that are painful, even overwhelming.

We tend to paint a rosier picture about the good old days, when now is the only time we have to grow into the person we're meant to become. The past, good or bad, is over. Many people ask me what I think of the benefits of working through your pain from the past. I believe there is a great tendency to add pain by dwelling on what we've been through, causing us to feel sorry for ourselves. When we concentrate our energies on all the sorrow and tragedy, this is literally dangerous to our mental and physical health.

We must use our minds to think the thoughts that are going to empower us, that mirror what we want to manifest in our lives. Instead of saying, "I've been through this awful situation," be proud of your inner strength and be glad that you handled everything so well. We must all try hard not to get stuck in the past. The bad or good old days are not nowadays. We're here, not there. We can choose to open our mind and heart to what is now possible, real, and right for us under the present circumstances.

A young mother with screaming small children can't imagine that this too will pass. Nothing is ever as bad or as good as we think. Things can always get worse or better—and they often do. The sick baby becomes a healthy teenager. The husband you loved for decades is dead and you can't bring him back to life. The big family house is no longer appropriate for you to live in alone. You're no longer allowed to drive because of failing eyesight. Your back and knee problems keep you from playing tennis. You always loved having Thanksgiving at home; now your family is scattered all over the country and they have chosen to have their own traditional holiday in their own homes. We have to honor this decision, be grateful for all the years we were under one roof together, and move on.

If you vowed you would never get a divorce, yet you married the wrong person—your spouse wasn't happy with you or vice versa—and you find yourself divorced and alone, this is the real situation now. You can't force someone to love you, be faithful to you, or be attracted to you. Look upon your life now as your fresh start, a clean slate.

An interpretation of the Buddha's teachings: "In the end these things matter most: How well did you love? How fully did you live? How deeply did you learn to let go? Let go. Why cling to the pain and the wrongs of yesterday? Why hold on to the very things that keep you from hope and love?"

What you can't change and improve, try not to carry on your shoulders. Shortly after my twin grandchildren, Nicholas and Anna, were born, a friend lost all three of her grandchildren in a tragic plane crash. Her son-in-law had chartered a small private plane to take his children to the Grand Canyon and it crashed and everyone died. When I heard this news, I was devastated. The next time I saw my friend, she gave me a catalogue of children's clothing from England: "These are the best, most tasteful clothes for grandchildren." Once, when Suzanne talked about her loss, she said she will never get over the tragedy. It is so unnatural to lose a child or a grandchild, but she said she accepts what she can't change and doesn't look back at what might have been.

The ancient Greek philosopher Epictetus popularized the Stoic ethical doctrine of limiting one's desires and believed that one should act in life as at a banquet by taking a polite portion of all that is offered. "He is a wise man who does not grieve for the things which he has not, but rejoices for those which he has."

Tragic losses are the hardest to accept. Losing a child is the worst of all possible losses. Losing our parents and our siblings is extremely painful. When our friends die, we are reminded of our own mortality. Life on earth is about love and loss. We live with uncertainty. We never know what is going to happen from one moment to the next, but "Without freedom from the past," the Indian spiritual leader Krishnamurti teaches us, "there is no freedom at all, because the mind is never new, fresh, innocent." When we don't let go and move on, we put a shadow over the light of the present.

I believe each one of us has the inner resources to deal with whatever life presents to us, no matter how unspeakably sad. As a parent, as a mother, it is not always easy to let go, to know that my children are now grown, and there's nothing I can do but be loving when they're going and growing through inevitable difficulties. It's hard not to interfere or to worry, but I have to choose to move on so they are free to figure things out on their own. Situations will continue to change for all of us, and each of us has to make our own tough choices that will bring us and others the greatest good.

When we make the best of what we now have, we live with fewer regrets. We're able to make the commitment to let go and move on. When the former NBC top news anchor Tom Brokaw willingly left his job in November 2004, he graciously said, "Life is filled with seasons. And this is a different season."

All our well-lived experiences give us the strength to move on to the next season, the next chapter, the next choice that will be the most appropriate and noble. Ultimately, we choose to be as loving and compassionate as possible to ourselves and others, understanding that we are all connected in this evolving life journey. We are all moving on, letting go of what's over. This collective consciousness of our interconnectedness, of our children being parents, of our grandchildren growing up, helps us to be courageous and to deepen our love of life. When we're given the baton, we make the best music we can while it is in our hands. And when it is time to pass it on to the next generation, glad for the part we played in the whole orchestration of life, we move on and let others have an opportunity to shine without any shadows. Whenever we move on, we stay in the light of the good life, well lived.

I make the most of all that comes and the least of all that goes.

SARA TEASDALE

Walk Away

Do you think that anybody can damage your soul?
Then why are you so embarrassed? I laugh at those who
think they can damage me. They do not know who I am,
they do not know what I think, they cannot even touch the
things which are really mine and with which I live.

EPICTETUS

There is a wooden sign at the Water Street Café oyster bar, a favorite local restaurant: "Be nice or leave." My reaction to people who are mean-spirited is to try to avoid them at all costs. Sometimes they are unavoidable, and we find ourselves with someone who is not kind. What is our choice? How can we set our own boundaries, keep our self-esteem, not sell our souls, and be true to what's most important inside us when we are in the presence of someone who is not nice? How can we keep our self-respect when someone we're with is disrespectful and antagonistic?

The wisest choice we can make is not to be dragged down. Don't accept someone who tries to take your dignity away. There are people we come in contact with, in business and social interactions, who have a chip on their shoulder. They are so insecure; they pretend they are superior. They can be extremely rude and say horrible things.

I'm often told by people seeking advice that the people they work with are nasty, negative, they hate their job, and they obviously hate themselves. Because there is no way we can ever change another human being, our only right choice is to walk away. There are other jobs. We are not slaves to bad energy. If we work for a creepy boss who has the wrong values, it is possible that he or she could also be dishonest, doing things that are not appropriate or good. Quit the job. It is just a job. Your life is worth more than a paycheck. Once we realize we are not a helpless victim, that this situation is not right or normal but is unhealthy and could be dangerous, we realize we have a choice: We can say, "Don't take me there." Life is too precious. If you are not in a position to quit your job or if the difficult person is a relative or spouse or neighbor, choose to protect yourself by keeping your distance as best you can when this person is misbehaving.

If someone insults you or provokes you in any way, or is abrupt and rude and impolite, avoid a conflict. Sometimes you can literally walk away. At other times, turn the other cheek, and don't fight back. If someone complains to you about your mother or daughter or friend, you can simply say, "I don't want to hear about it."

The ultimate way to live a good life is to surround yourself with superior people who set a great example for you to follow. Unhappy people will be unhappy wherever they are. When they are with you, they will be unhappy. That is where they are. They have not yet chosen to do the painful inner work of training their minds to improve their attitude. That is their choice. Your choice is to remain pure and clean and bright, and to remain loving in your energy. This is an important form of self-protection and self-preservation. In extreme cases, you may have to avoid all communication to protect your soul.

You are not helping miserable people by tolerating their behavior. Set limits. Maintain your standards. Recognize that being grumpy and gruff and mean is not acceptable to you under any circumstances. Our daughter Brooke loves to say, "Don't spoil my Zen." It's not just in what people say, but also in their tone of voice, in what they don't say, in their cold eyes, and their dismissive or condescending manner toward you. That energy is toxic. Choose not to try to win some people over. The good life is not a popularity contest. Bad people are not good, they are not nice, and they are not going to easily reform. Far better to be loving and walk away. "Be nice or leave." Sometimes it's the best choice to be nice and leave.

> Speak the affirmative: emphasize your choice by
> utter ignoring of all you reject.
>
> **EMERSON**

See the Big in the Little

Do not wait . . . be happy if one little thing leads to progress, and reflect on the fact that what results from such a little thing is not, in fact, so very little.

MARCUS AURELIUS

There is nothing little that isn't, in some way, connected to something big. A microcosm is a small representative system that has analogies to a larger system in construction, configuration, and development. A macrocosm is the entire world, the universe. We are persuaded, more and more, that virtually everything is connected. When we seek and find the connections, we come to better understand the process of transformation. We can be more mindful and try to become more aware of the phenomenon observable over time.

Look at the miracle of a snowflake. Like a snowflake, each one of us is uniquely beautiful, symmetrical, and perfect. We understand how fragile a snowflake is, but when it is joined by billions and billions of other snowflakes, it can be part of a blizzard. One drop of rain united with billions and billions of other drops of rain can become a storm or a hurricane and cause severe damage when combined with high winds, high tides, and flooding.

We can put grass seed in the soil, knowing that the rain or our watering, combined with the rays of sun, will cause these tiny seeds to sprout and form a lovely green grass lawn.

We live in the world of a snowflake and a drop of water. We see, close up, the small, the details, the parts, the elements. These small, subtle items or parts are all enormously significant. Without them the whole cannot exist. It's important to regularly pause in order to reflect on the micro becoming the macro. When we're able to step outside our routine, observing things from a broad perspective, we can become astonished by the proverbial world in a grain of sand.

Each of us has approximately 100 trillion cells in our body. Every human cell has intelligence, or DNA. We each house a universe. The author Robert Wright, who has a knack for understanding and explaining scientific mysteries, in *The Moral Animal* wrote that " . . . nuances can start intellectual avalanches." The smallest shift in our minds can cause a momentous insight. The smallest kindness at a dark time can light up a life. It's important to know that a smile helps someone who is grieving. The same power holds true for an unkindness that can cause someone a great deal of pain. Nothing is little. Everything has great and lasting significance for better or for worse. We should never underestimate the power of music to uplift our spirit. We can read a brief powerful poem that can change our life.

Krishnamurti wisely instructs us, "You must understand the whole of life, not just one little part of it. That is why you must read, that is why you must look at skies, that is why you must sing, and dance, and write poems, and suffer, and understand, for all that is life." Everything affects our soul. There is great value in whatever happens.

While you're doing the least of things, envision the most of things. See the big in the little so you can make sure you are moving in the direction of your ideal. We can put our whole heart, our mind and soul, into the smallest acts. We can fully engage our five senses. We can keep our mind alert, knowing that there is something major in every minor thing that happens to us and around us. Every moment of being is essential in the process of our becoming.

Lao Tzu taught us to embrace the one. "The way to do," he said, "is to be." In stillness and calm contemplation, the seeds of great accomplishments are germinating. Feel this sense of wholeness and integration. Enthusiastically participate in all the little things that make life happy. Too many people are task-oriented, whirling around with one long *to do* list. But when we begin to see the interconnection of all things, what we think and do takes on a deeper, more significant meaning.

Think of the energy of the extended hands, the labor of love, which creates music, art, and literature; think of a mother touching a child; think of all the tenderness that is central to our life. As a discipline, as you engage in little daily tasks, think of the other people who help make your life possible. If you were to bake your own bread, it would take you approximately four hours. Think of the process that went into the bread: first, the wheat is sowed and the sun and the rain work their magic. Then the wheat is harvested and trucked to a factory where it is made into flour. Then the flour is made into dough. The bread is baked, wrapped, and sent to the market. When you are aware of the process, you appreciate all the things that went right in order for you to see that fresh loaf on the shelf. Many people were involved in making this loaf of bread.

When you make a sandwich for a child's lunch, it is good to think of the farmer who grew the wheat, and the baker who made the loaf of bread. When you make coffee in the morning, think of the coffee growers and pickers. We're all part of a chain of interlocking connections. The mug I use for my coffee is from Brittany, France, hand-painted in a factory by artists. I can envision them decorating the mug to make it more attractive. I am grateful for their care and effort that now enrich my life.

There is a cute elderly couple at a booth in the farmers' market who are relative newlyweds. They both lost their spouses and were married a few years ago. They sell corn. Their crude handwritten sign says FRESH CORN 50¢ AN EAR. The wife, Velora, thinks her favorite variety, "Serendipity," is sweeter than her husband's "Butter and Sugar" corn. They always sell out by mid-morning. Everyone wants to give Whit and Velora their business because they are so adorable. She sits, he stands behind her, in their matching red aprons. Their interchange is so sweet. He always wants to discount the price because there just might be a worm somewhere. She instructs people how to cook the corn: "Bring the water to a full boil after putting the corn in and boil for five to eight minutes." Whit adds, "Test it with a fork." "Pay no attention. He's not the corn cooker, he's the corn grower." Everyone laughs.

We buy zinnias from an adjacent farmer's booth. Just seeing these bright fuchsia, orange, and yellow flowers brings me back to Rippy's Market in Westport, where my brother Powell used to pick zinnias for Mr. Rippy for extra money as a teenager. Life is far more interesting when we awaken these associations, memories, and thoughts of the unknown others who do their little and big jobs faithfully so the world operates in some sort of cooperation. So many people are involved in our lives, seen and unseen. Think of all that goes right. Let your mind expand in the attitude of abundance, taking in all our imagination allows. John Keats, the British poet, wrote in the early nineteenth century, "I do not live in this world alone, but in a thousand worlds."

Albert Einstein felt deeply grateful for all the people who sustained his life. He felt obligated to play his part. He believed, "There are only two ways to live your life: One is as though nothing is a miracle. The other is as though everything is a miracle." I'm told that 84 percent of Americans believe in miracles. Do you? Little things can excite awe and wonder. Emerson wants us to understand: "The invariable mark of wisdom is to see the miraculous in the common." The best way not to get caught up in *chores,* doing mundane things that bog us down, is to find meaning and purpose in everything. Choose to see the miraculous in a drop of water, a grain of sand, a snowflake, a soap bubble, a flower, the tenderness of love, the sun, the moon, the stars. Equally awesome is our being alive to experience all the big in all the little.

Awe enables us to perceive in the world intimations of the divine, to sense in small things the beginning of infinite significance, to sense the ultimate in the common and the simple; to feel in the rush of the passing the stillness of the eternal.

RABBI ABRAHAM JOSHUA HESCHEL

40

Surround Yourself with People You Trust

Trust men and they will be true to you; treat them greatly
and they will show themselves great.

EMERSON

Make trust a foundation of all your choices. The way to lasting happiness is trust. Goethe assured us that "As soon as you trust yourself, you will know how to live." The beginning of trusting the integrity of someone else is to find your own character and to be worthy of others' trust. Self-trust builds the self-confidence and self-respect that lead you to trust others.

If someone is a cheat, he believes everyone else is cheating, too. What we believe to be true matters. How do honest people manage to survive in the Darwinian jungle of competition? The honest man might lose the race to the dishonest challenger. But in the rest of life, honesty always rings true and is hard to fake.

People who are scrupulously honest are far more eligible for important jobs where trust is a prerequisite. When people shade the truth, cut corners, round off numbers, and, in a variety of ways, take advantage of others, they will ultimately suffer. They won't be offered better positions or promotions. Once caught, they will lose their credibility and perhaps their job. But, more important, our soul insists on purity or we suffer real harm. Any dishonesty takes the light from our soul and we lose our integrity.

Life is far too short to spend time with shady people. Judge your own character by the people you deal with. Everyone's *not* doing it. What's more, humans seem to be able to sense cheaters. Robert Frank, an economist at the Johnson Graduate School of Management at Cornell University and the author of *What Price the Moral High Ground?*, wrote an article in the *New York Times* entitled, "There's a Hidden Price for Being a Cheat," about an experiment involving a game of trust: "Strangers of only brief acquaintance were asked to predict which of their partners would cheat them. The players they identified were more than twice as likely as others to be cheaters." How trusting are you in general? Do you believe you are a good, accurate judge of someone's character? Can you tell when people are trying to take advantage of you?

When I played competitive tennis, I always tried to play with people who were better than I was so I could improve my game. Not only did my tennis improve, but the experience was far more exhilarating. Ideally, we should always try to associate with noble people; people who lift our game.

Aristotle believed that the people you associate with are reflections of yourself. If someone proves untrustworthy, irresponsible, and unreliable, and you don't believe what he says is true, you may have to choose to break off your relationship. Admit you made an honest mistake. Once trust is violated, you can forgive but not forget. There is no way to have healthy relationships with people who slant the truth. If you can't rely on people, you can't relate to them. To believe in someone, we must trust they are telling us the truth.

Think of all the people who put their firm reliance on the intention and integrity of someone only to find the person cheats on them. Why do so many people continue to stick around? They get used to the person. Don't get used to bad behavior.

Fundamental trust in good people carries you through. But remember you don't have to bring everyone into your inner circle. Trust your judgment. When my daughters were young, they would say, "Trust me." And I did. But I also realize that trust is earned. We have to trust, but there are times when caution is the right choice.

Love all, trust a few, do wrong to none.

SHAKESPEARE

Intuition Is Your Guiding Light

The great decisions of human life have as a rule far more to do
with the instincts and other mysterious unconscious factors than
with conscious will and well-meaning reasonableness.

CARL JUNG

Because intuition is not scientific or concrete, some people are unaware of its presence. Intuition is unproven insight, a supernatural element of experience, an awakening to the divine spirit that exists inside us and that is outside of the natural world, part of the whole universal intelligence. When we are in a state of higher consciousness, quieting our mind, we know things to be true intuitively; we follow our gut, this inner good knowing.

Taking things in through our rational minds prepares us for insight, instinct, and intuition. With the keen perception of our five senses, we activate our brain's pathways of knowing. Some people think of intuition as a third eye, connecting the right brain and the left brain. Others think of intuition as our sixth sense, a mystical way of knowing. Our sensuous knowing, along with the rational processes of our minds, helps us go into the center of our being, to a place that senses and knows. This inner vision is wisdom. We're often able to intuit the truth long before we have any proof by way of reason; we just know something is right or wrong.

My consulting of several dictionaries yielded these definitions of intuition: the act or faculty of knowing or sensing without the use of rational processes; immediate knowing—a quick, ready, perceptive insight, a sense of something not evident or detectable—a sharp impression. Intuition is essentially instinctive and is followed by intelligence.

Why is it that a sharp insight comes to you while washing your hair in the shower? Intuition comes to a prepared mind, fine spun from a quiet mind, at peace. We nourish our intuition in moments of silence, when we go inward, as when we're in the most beautiful natural settings. In moments of contemplation, we feel a presence, a sense of harmony, an insight that comes to us. Intuition is mysterious, invisible, intangible and, for the most part, indescribable.

Emerson was a transcendentalist. A literary and philosophical movement, transcendentalism was concerned with the intuitive basis of knowledge as independent of experience. It asserted that a fundamental spiritual ideal transcends the empirical and scientific. Emerson strongly stated, "I can accept nothing unless I feel it intuitively." I believe that many of us know this to be the truth for us, but it is often hard to follow something as elusive as our guiding light. Intuition goes beyond common thought or experience.

We're not all born with the same intuitive capability to discern the true nature of things, but we can all nurture our natural inclinations. When we acknowledge our intuitive powers, we are not denying our minds. But when we don't tap into our intuition, we are only half alive. The benefits of intuition can make an enormous difference in how we make choices that will allow us to live as well as humanly possible. Consider how intuition can benefit your search for a good life.

William Spear, a wise feng shui expert and author, teaches us about the invisible energies present in all things. Just because we can't fully comprehend something as puzzling as ultimate reality doesn't mean it doesn't exist. "Intuition," Spear teaches, "is like a magnet, guided by the clear, unblocked stream of energy that flows between heaven and earth along our spine."

Our consciousness of our self and our environment is only half awake if we don't embrace the transcendental and metaphysical. Only then can we go beyond our thinking into pure *being*. These glimpses of unity cannot easily be talked about or described. Poets sometimes come closest, but it is not necessary to share these moments of pure intuitive knowing with anyone. Perhaps we should think of intuition as the great gift that guides us into pure light, pure awareness, pure boundless mysteries, wonder and joy. When we are alone in this timeless, space-less, pure potential state, we will never be lonely; we will come to trust this guiding spirit, this great source of inspiration. We will always find our way home.

A final thought from someone who thought so well, who understood the power of mystery and wonder that are fundamental to true art and science. Albert Einstein concluded: "He who can no longer wonder, can no longer feel amazement, is as good as dead, a snuffed out candle."

Say yes: choose intuition as your guiding light. You don't have to know where it comes from or how it all works. Just be grateful you have this powerful gift within your soul.

> The divine spirit is inside of us. If it were not, the power
> to be good would be beyond our reach.

SENECA

Never Say Never

To change one's mind in changing circumstances is true wisdom.

ROBERT LOUIS STEVENSON

Of one thing I am certain, I will never say never again. Every time I have said never, I've been wrong. The classic example was when a publisher and editor arranged a luncheon with my literary agent, Carl Brandt, and me. There, at a favorite restaurant of the literary and publishing group, over a delicious lobster salad, I turned down their proposal to write three decorating books. I put my fork down and without looking at Carl, I said, "I will never write another decorating book." Carl almost choked, could have kicked me under the table, and tenderly said, "Sandie, never say never. You never can be sure." Several years later, I was given a three-book contract and went on to write three of my best decorating books, *The Decoration of Houses*, *Open Your Eyes*, and *Feeling at Home*.

None of us can ever be sure of anything. Keep an open mind. Different circumstances require different choices. Never is forever and leaves no flexibility, no wiggle room, no balance. Peter's decision never to marry again left me no hope. We were friends, and he'd chosen not to try his hand at marriage again after his first two failed. But when John Coburn counseled us before marrying us in 1974, he told Peter (with a wink and a smile), that he was now experienced in love and could be an ideal partner for me. In Peter's unsuccessful search for lasting union with a soul mate, he'd decided not to marry; but when my daughter Brooke, at age four, "proposed," he realized that perhaps it would be in a marriage to me that what had eluded him in the past was now possible. Peter asked me to marry him at dinner that night and told me he'd never loved anyone more. Later he explained what had enlightened him was his experience with the Central Park carousel where, as a young rider, he discovered that in the whirl around, the golden ring was offered to the rider—if at all—just once.

Anyone pretends who speculates that they know what the future will bring. The French writer Simone de Beauvoir said, "I tore myself away from the safe comfort of certainties through my love of truth, and truth rewarded me." Try not to say you'll never outgrow certain beliefs because saying so will close your mind, when you are obviously searching for guidance and direction. There are many roads to truth, and some of them are not the best paved or marked; they are stumbled upon unexpectedly.

Peter had a roommate at Yale, the Class of '44, who died during World War II. One evening when Peter and Donald Twining were in their room studying, Donald looked up from his book and exclaimed to Peter, "Around the corner of every moment is the fascination of the unknown." Peter has never forgotten that profound statement. Because we never know, we should feel the freedom that comes from acceptance. We step into the unknown, accepting what comes, and letting go of what goes. Choose to change your mind when circumstances change and when you've evolved to greater depth and understanding. I'm grateful Peter stopped saying never.

The heart has reasons which the reason cannot understand.

BLAISE PASCAL

Every cause produces more than one effect.

HERBERT SPENCER

Every choice we make has far-reaching consequences; all actions do. I'm a great believer in the universal principle of cause and effect. What we sow we reap. Every action has a reaction. What goes around comes around. All the old sayings are true. If someone is dull, his dreary behavior causes dreary feelings in others. If someone is stimulating and inspired, they have an infectious way of exciting and inspiring others. When we give the best we have to give, the best comes back to us; in some way we are rewarded. It may not be in exactly the way we expect, but the more we put into life, the more we get out of it, the more good we experience. We've been taught since early childhood that it is better to give than to receive. The great secret we grow to discover is that the more we give, the more we possess, or have inwardly.

Lao Tzu, believed to be the founder of Taoism, understood the law of cause and effect and wrote, "Having given all he had, he then is very rich indeed." You receive more than you give when you do good deeds.

Cause and effect is a scientific principle. When an apple falls from a tree because of gravity, where it will land can be determined. Every action, each mindset, has consequences. If you set a table in an angry consciousness, or feed a child in a grumpy mood, it hurts you and the people you are feeding. Energy, good and bad, affects us. In Hinduism and Buddhism, we are taught that every deed or action has a cause and effect, that we have a distinctive aura, an atmosphere, that surrounds us in our thinking, feeling, and actions.

The seventeenth-century Dutch philosopher Spinoza taught, "Nothing exists from whose nature some effect does not follow." Each choice we make will make a difference, for better or worse.

Determine the value of an action by weighing it against the value of its consequences. The term for this is consequentialism. Consider the logical consequence of every action. You and I have the power to produce an action that will achieve a good result. We have a great deal of influence about the way we live our lives. The author of *Anatomy of an Illness,* Norman Cousins, believed, "Wisdom consists of anticipation of consequences." We choose what we want to produce. The Swiss psychiatrist Carl Jung wrote in *Psychological Reflections,* "Man breathes his own life into things until finally they begin to live of themselves and to multiply." We are the ones who choose our life's course. The best way to get the most out of our short lifetimes is to put forth more effort. Our lives are made possible by the goodwill and hard work of so many others. We first have to give, in order to receive the full measure of abundance of all the good things in life.

Choose wisely what actions of others you will pay attention to and those you will ignore. Be sure your actions will bring the results you desire. When you are responsible for the consequences of your actions, when you are never satisfied with what you have done, but are dedicated to doing more and better, you will be making a useful, worthwhile contribution to the universe. In turn, you will be awarded abundantly for your good work.

You are your choices; you choose what you want to manifest with the best-intended results. If you choose the path that leads you to the good life, you will be living in the light. This is just common sense.

Cause and effect are two sides of one fact.

Shallow men believe in luck or in circumstance.
Strong men believe in cause and effect.

What you see comes to you.

The current of inward life increases as it is spent.

EMERSON

Choose Love for Yourself and Others

What's the earth
With all its art, verse, music, worth—
Compared with love, found, gained, and kept?

Take away love, and our earth is a tomb.

ROBERT BROWNING

Love is a force for good; being loving is a commitment. This powerful, often misunderstood energy can change the world. Who and what we love defines us. We become beautiful when we are loving and are loved by others. We choose to be loving and lovable. We make ourselves worthy of love.

We have a giant capacity to love. What we need to do to increase love's power and to spread more joy to others is to cultivate and maintain a strong love of self. If we don't deeply love our self, it is not possible to be genuinely loving to others. And when we don't really like and love who we are, it is harder for others to find us lovable. People will withdraw their love from us if our essential nature is unloving. The first, most necessary, and good choice is to go inside and examine your own conscience: do you operate from a loving consciousness?

When we are in a loving consciousness, we are full of sunshine and light, we smile easily, and our joy spreads in all directions. We can never love too much when loving is genuine. The sage Lao Tzu taught us to be empty and be full. The paradox is that in order to fill our hearts with sunshine and effervescent loving energy, we have to empty ourselves of anger, frustration, hatred, and any negative thoughts and judgments that stand in the way of our own light.

People who honor themselves respect the dignity of others. Many of my readers challenge me when I emphasize the need to center ourselves first in order to be able to tenderly care for the needs of our loved ones. Self-love is not egotism; it is a commitment to let the loving light of truth radiate from the center of our being.

Love is the invisible force for good that is in our human heart. If everyone loved himself more, there would be less need for hospitals; there would be more peace around the world. If we cloud over our true nature, we begin to die inside. Someone who truly loves himself will not knowingly and deliberately try to harm another person. Our responsibility as individuals on this planet is to seek and find greater ways to love ourselves, to love life more spaciously, and to love and serve others more compassionately. Understanding love is sometimes complex, but it is the most essential of all endeavors on the path toward the good life.

The spiritual philosopher Stephen Mitchell wrote: "The heart is like a window." Our love resides in our hearts. We must clean our windows to let the sunlight, air, view, stars, and moon inside. Think of your heart as infinite and boundless with billions and trillions of windows, wondrously spacious, exposing you to the most breathtakingly beautiful scenery you could possibly imagine. Everything pretty you've ever seen you still see in this luminous inner chamber of your open heart. Every wonderful experience you've ever had lives inside you. Whenever we neglect our self, our windows become dirty, we can't see out as clearly; we are indirectly being less loving to others because we haven't done our inner work, we haven't kept our windows clean.

Love is our vital force, our fuel, our energy, our power. The more we love, the more we have to give. The supply is unlimited as long as we fill up our own well—our heart—every day. In order to keep your heart pure, full of radiant love, every morning when you awaken, commit yourself to choose to be more loving to yourself and others. Charles Schulz, the creator of *Peanuts*, came to the conclusion that "There's nothing worse than being unloved." I agree and add that there's nothing worse than being unloved because it means we are being unloving. People are starved for genuine love. We're attracted to it and we're able to share this blessing.

I'm a fan of the romantic poet Robert Browning. The marriage between him and his beloved wife Elizabeth Barrett is a love story that has been well documented in their poems. Not all of us are poets, but we can strongly believe in the transforming power of love. Nothing is more wonderful or feels better than pure, unconditional love.

You should always be able to be yourself in a loving relationship. The sociologist and psychoanalyst Erich Fromm, the author of *The Art of Loving*, wrote, "Love is union with somebody, or something, outside oneself, under the condition of retaining the separateness and integrity of one's own self." The love we generate and increase will help us to understand ourselves and others better. The depth of our wisdom is measured by how openly and profoundly we love ourselves, our lives, and others. When we are loving, we give our best to everything we do because our hearts and souls are our truest guides.

Love heals us. The cancer doctor and author Bernie Siegel understands: "When you affirm your life, you give everyone who comes in contact with you a gift, and you find your immortality in the love you leave behind." Try to do everything in the spirit of love that will activate and bring out all the bright forces within you. We are made more beautiful, more lovable, when we smile. Every kind and tender thought we have will help our heart to sing.

Choose to be more loving to yourself and others. This is the wisest choice you can make because joy and happiness will be your spirit-energy. As I said in my book *Living in Love*, love is both sublime and divine.

Whatever you want to do in this lifetime can be done, and you can accomplish anything you want, as long as you have enough love in your heart. If you are not getting what you are trying to get, just add a little extra love, and you will get it.

DEEPAK CHOPRA

Do More Things That Make You Happy

Where your pleasure is, there is your treasure; where your treasure, there your heart; where your heart, there your happiness.

SAINT AUGUSTINE

Sometimes the obvious escapes us. Whenever we're enjoying what we're doing, we'll do a better job, have more fun, and feel a certain sense of ease, delight, and mastery. We become better at something because of the time we spend doing it. I read somewhere that if we were to spend two hours a day doing something that we choose to do that makes us happy, within five years we can become an expert at it.

The researcher and author on the state of flow Mihaly Csikszentmihalyi believes, "It is essential to learn to enjoy life. It really does not make sense to go through the motions of existence if one does not appreciate as much of it as possible." We, and we alone, are in charge of discovering and then deciding what we want to do more of that will make us happy. There are certain things we have to do that are necessary and appropriate. I believe we can choose to find ways to do even these things with greater pleasure and satisfaction by making a commitment to making the best out of every situation.

I love what actress Katharine Hepburn's mother advised her: "If you always do what interests you, at least one person is pleased." A lot of conscientious people think they aren't meant to concern themselves with their own happiness when they are trying to help others. But if we want others to be happy, we certainly can set an example as we go about helping others live better lives.

Marcus Aurelius concluded, "Very little is needed to make a happy life." In 1960, I met a missionary couple in Madras, India, whose wisdom increased my understanding of happiness enormously. I was curious how they were able to be so comfortable, have such inner peace, and feel such joy when their living conditions were so primitive. The Donnellys smiled and told me, "When we have our favorite books, fresh flowers, meaningful work, and the companionship of each other, this is all we need to be happy."

Many of us lead extremely complicated lives and at times we feel overwhelmed by the weight of responsibility. In this state of imbalance, it is easy to lose our direction. We merely do the best we can to go through the motions and are glad we're able to get events behind us. There are times in all of our lives when we have to focus on sad and painful situations. But in the big picture, when life is running more smoothly, we have to remember to get back in the habit of making choices that will provide opportunities for us to do more and more things that make us happy.

Pay close attention to how you feel when you are in the swing of activity. What things do you enjoy doing that make you feel most alive? What do you want to do more of? Try to spend as much time as possible doing activities that you find exhilarating. Claude Monet said, "Perhaps, I owe it to flowers to be a painter," meaning he was good for two things— painting and gardening. In truth, he also was passionate about food, but he hired others to cook for him. He was busy painting. We can't do everything. We have to choose. No one could paint for Monet. He chose to make painting the center of his life, surrounded by his family and garden. Just because we love delicious food doesn't mean we have to cook every meal ourselves unless it makes us happy to do so.

I'm fascinated to learn from people of great accomplishment what choices they've made to do things that bring them great fulfillment. Thomas Jefferson, in his older years, took up gardening, claiming he was a young gardener. The mythology teacher and writer Joseph Campbell followed his bliss by going off to the wilderness for five years to read.

A woman who lives in Annapolis, Maryland, is a court reporter who paddles her kayak to work in the morning. Our neighbor Charles dives off a friend's dock across the street every day that the temperature isn't freezing. His usual comment is, "It's perfect. You should come in." When people feel pleasure from what they do, they want to share the joy with others. Their happiness is contagious.

We all have our own things we love to do. The things you love to do are not necessarily what I choose to do. But we must all proceed to do the things that make us happy.

When we continue to do more things that make us happier, we will become happier. This gift of well-being is the great reward of living the good life.

Each of us has a choice about how to love the world in our unique way.

It is the experience of living that is important, not searching for meaning. We bring meaning by how we love the world.

BERNIE SIEGEL

Trust Your Subjective Well-Being

We should know what our convictions are, and stand for them.
Upon one's own philosophy, conscious or unconscious, depends
one's ultimate interpretation of facts. Therefore it is wise to be
as clear as possible about one's subjective principles. As the
man is, so will be his ultimate truth.

CARL JUNG

How many of us are brave enough to admit how we really feel? Very few, I'm afraid. As thinking, sensitive adults, we should be able to follow our actual feelings. Women tend to feel guilty when they have everything in the world to make them happy, yet they sense that something is missing. People tell us how fortunate and blessed we are with the outer trappings of a good life, when what is really happening is something quite different. You can't be happy with things that "ought" to make you happy. That is a trap.

There is your inner self, the real truth, not the myth. A famous line from an utterly frustrated husband, "Why can't you be happy being a wife and mother?" could be answered, "Why can't you be happy being a husband and father?"

Sigmund Freud, the Austrian physician and founder of psychoanalysis, is not someone I admire. He theorized that the symptoms of hysterical patients represent forgotten and unresolved infantile psychosexual conflicts. He once complained that after studying women for over thirty years, he couldn't, for the life of him, figure out what they wanted. In one of his textbooks, he states that he wants women to be less hysterically unhappy.

In January 2005 *Time* magazine published a special issue on mind and body topics: "The Science of Happiness—Why optimists live longer. Is joy in your genes? Does God want us to be happy? Why we need to laugh." A Nobel Prize–winning psychologist, Daniel Kahneman of Princeton University, unveiled a new tool for assessing happiness called "The day-reconstructive method." He and his team of researchers asked participants to fill out a long diary and questionnaire detailing everything they'd done on the previous day, including people they were with. According to *Time* reporter Claudia Wallis, the participants were asked to rate a range of feelings during each episode they listed, such as whether they were happy, impatient, depressed, worried, tired, and so on. A group of 900 women in Texas were tested and the results were surprising: the five most positive activities listed by these women were sex, socializing, relaxing, praying or meditating, and eating. Exercising and watching television were not far behind. Way down on the list was taking care of children, which ranked below cooking, and only slightly above housework.

These findings were surprising because women frequently cite their children as their biggest source of delight (as indicated in a happiness poll conducted a month previous to this study). When asked, "What one thing in life has brought you the greatest happiness?", 35 percent of the women polled responded that their children or grandchildren, or both, were their greatest joy. "Spouse" was far behind at just 9 percent.

Based on this type of discrepancy between global reports on well-being ("My life is happy, and my children are my greatest joy"), compared to more specific data on enjoyment of day-to-day experiences ("What a night! The kids were such a pain!!"), scientists are discovering that there is a distinction between the *experienced self* and the *remembered self.* We should try to pay more careful attention to our actual experiences and emotions, rather than those colored by memory. Parents, especially mothers, are supposed to love taking caring of their children, but obviously many don't, even though they feel their children bring them their greatest joy.

Subjective well-being (SWB) is shaped by our unique personality, a blend of inborn temperament and environmental influences. Don't tell someone he ought to be happy eating cake when he feels like eating a piece of watermelon.

If you are an extrovert, you will tend to enjoy and need more interaction with others than if you are an introvert. If you're an optimist and have high self-esteem, you will have high SWB. We have biological setpoints of emotional experience. Circumstances change, but our dispositions remain fairly stable unless we make a serious effort to alter our natural attitude. The better your environment fits your personality, the greater your SWB. I had an interior design client who married a wealthy real estate broker. They had four children and lived in an elegant triplex. Shelby tried hard to fit into the mold, but discovered it was impossible. She ended up getting a divorce, entered the ministry, and works with prisoners. She's happy. The high-profile social life, the lavish entertaining, the expectations and pressure on her to live a moneyed lifestyle didn't fit her temperament or her values.

Be highly subjective. What's taking place in your mind and emotions is far more vitally informative than the external trappings of your life. When we are moved by true emotion, we often experience physiological changes—we get goose bumps or we cry or we feel that creepy-crawly feeling in our arms, or we get a stomach ache or chest pains. The truth is your subjective experience. If it is the most beautiful day out and you feel awful, it will not be as beautiful a day to you as to someone who has high SWB.

The whole concept of achieving the good life rarely varies among individuals. The path is the same for everyone. We have to seek and find what is true, good, and beautiful. For some, their ideal state is one of wealth, physical comforts, security, and luxury yet they are off their true path. For Shelby the good life was one of service to others. The ultimate guiding light to the good life is trusting your SWB.

From one to ten, how high would you rate your overall SWB? Don't feel guilty about being in touch with the depth of your feelings. You can always choose to make changes to improve your life. Knowing how you honestly feel is the only way you'll be able to make commonsense changes for the better. Does your environment suit your temperament? Do you feel free to make significant choices that you believe represent who you really are and how you, ideally, wish to live? How would you define the good life? If you say your life is satisfying, you are obviously experiencing many more pleasant experiences than unpleasant ones. When you feel well satisfied with your life, you are happy.

Rate your SWB in the various domains in your life from one to ten:

* Work

* Home

* Relationships

What are you striving for? If you want to become a physician, focus all your energy and resources toward that goal. If you want to excel in sports, doing so will increase your sense of happiness. Examine what your goals are so that you can make appropriate choices in pursuit of them.

What you feel is real. The best way to evaluate your life is to pay attention to the state of your mind and your heart. Don't look at what you have. We must try to look beneath the smooth surface of the pond. There may be an undertow of turbulence. Often people aren't consciously aware of what they like or want; many of us have learned to suppress our inner voice of truth.

As you are experiencing life, try to evaluate whether something is good or bad, as well as whether something makes you feel good or bad. Be aware of what you like, want, and need in the present. The psychiatrist Carl Rogers suggests we ask ourselves, "Am I living in a way which is deeply satisfying to me, and which truly expresses me?" We all yearn to be liked and loved. Most people feel the missing element in their happiness is love. We should love ourselves so completely that we value our SWB as an indicator of our inner fullness—our ability to give and receive love.

The goal is not to live *for* pleasure, but *with* pleasure. To know how to shape your environment to provide more positive stimulation is your task. Be true to your subjective well-being based on your heart's feelings. Be sure it's your life you're living.

> I have always found the idea of unconscious emotions extremely difficult to think about . . . as in most definitions of emotion . . . a subjective experience of feeling is an essential component.
>
> **PHOEBE ELLSWORTH**

47

Avoid Perfection in Pursuit of Excellence

Perfection is bogus.

TONI SCIARRA

All the ancient sages and philosophers teach us to perfect ourselves, to become more morally virtuous, more excellent. But perfectionism as a personality trait, when taken out of the context of the whole character of a person, is imbalanced and self-defeating. To strive to be a better person— more loving, compassionate, empathetic, understanding, kind, gentle, and generous—is honorable. When we genuinely want to live the good life, one of excellence and meaning, we will come to know that no human being can possibly perfect every aspect of himself in one brief lifetime.

A perfectionist is someone who has a propensity for being displeased with anything that is not perfect. With extremely high standards, forever seeking faultless, flawless, impeccable situations, perfectionists are chronically unhappy in the real world of tumble and rough. I often say, "Living is a messy business."

It is wise to strive, but it is also wise to know that it takes time and patience to turn a rough stone into a precious gem. We are imperfect; we have work to do. We are in the continuous state of becoming. When we focus on perfecting our inner light, when we work on raising our consciousness to new heights, we will see the process of becoming as our chief concern, our ideal purpose, and a perfect use of our energies. We can always excel and even exceed our former self when we aim at high standards.

There are far too many perfectionists, however, whose standards are dangerously high. Nothing on earth is ever perfect; it never was and never will be. We have to live with imperfection not only in people—ourselves, family members, friends, community, and the world—but in the objects we live with. One of the reasons I'm so naturally attracted to Thai silk is the irregularity of the weave. The fabric has great integrity and character because it is not consistent in the way it is hand woven.

When I sat on the board of the wonderful American textile company, Fieldcrest Cannon, I regularly went to different mills in North Carolina to experience the textile-making process. It's fascinating to see Egyptian cotton come in one end of a mill and shrink-wrapped bed linens come out the other end. I was terribly disappointed to learn how much money this great company lost on black sheets. If there was a tiny unnoticeable inconsistency in the cotton, the black dye wouldn't take evenly. For a pinprick "flaw" that could be on the bottom end where a sheet is tucked in, the sheet was marked a "second" and sold at a price less than it cost to make. A black sheet is expensive to make because white cotton becomes black through being saturated in black dye.

If there were fewer consumers who were perfectionists, picking things apart, perpetuating their own suffering and inflicting their unhappiness on others, more manufacturers could make an honest profit. People who live in a state of relentless perfectionism have developed maladaptive patterns of behavior. If someone believes that nothing they do is ever quite good enough, that it has to be perfect, nothing good comes out of them. There is a paralysis of heart, an inability to cope with the reality of everyday life. When the neighbor's apartment above ours sprung a leak that flooded our bathroom and laundry room, I had to live with the mess. It was not a perfect situation; it was reality. What's often real is not always ideal.

My advice to a perfectionist is to pay attention to all the good in his or her life. Look at all the fine and noble qualities in your spouse or partner. Rejoice in your children's intelligence, health, and energetic personalities.

Love your house and make it a real home just as it is now. The roof leaks, you need to paint the outside, the furniture is wearing out or faded—that's where you are now. No amount of money will ever be enough to someone who is never satisfied with the way things are.

The *New York Times* columnist and author David Brooks, in an interesting book, *On Paradise Drive: How We Live Now (and Always Have) in the Future Tense*, reveals some telling details about American cultural habits. I learned that one in three women in America dyes her hair, for example. Brooks writes, "Just beyond the next ridge, just with the next entrepreneurial scheme or diet plan; just with the next political hero, the next credit card purchase or the next true love, there is this spot you can get to where all the tensions will melt, all time pressures are relieved, and all contentment can be realized . . . This, my friend, is America."

People, places, and things are not perfect. Perfectionism can become an extreme mental disorder requiring hospitalization. Patients are trained to make up only half a bed, something paradoxical to say the least.

We are, in our essence, imperfect because we are human. Our humanity is what makes us strive to better ourselves, to chase after a full, rich, and happy life, to pursue higher education, gain skills, have goals, and choose excellence over mediocrity. Be proud of yourself when you excel, when you show superiority in your work, but try never to act superior to others. Learn to be satisfied when you do your best, even if it isn't ideal. Remember the principle of the Japanese flaw: all real beauty has some slight imperfection. The wonderful Romantic poet Robert Browning understood: "What comes to perfection perishes." Nothing that is perfect lasts for long. Be grateful for a perfect kiss or a perfect rest or a perfect cookie. Carl Brandt, my literary agent and friend, believes there are no perfect answers; the perfect answer is the truth. I believe the perfect answer comes closest to the truth.

Goethe taught us, "Higher aims are in themselves more valuable, even if unfulfilled, than lower ones quite attained." Aim high and then enjoy the pleasure of the process of getting there. The charming actor Maurice Chevalier warned us, "If you wait for the perfect moment when all is safe and assured, it may never arrive. Mountains will not be climbed, races won, or lasting happiness achieved."

As we make this commitment to pursue excellence, keep in mind that we are not seeking perfection, we are interested in living the good life of balance:

* Although you may have less than perfect health, you can live a full and productive life.

* You will never know ultimate truths entirely.

* Enjoying old clothes that show signs of wear and tear is good for your soul.

* Decorating your house is an active process; there is no finishing, only making things more charming, inviting, and comfortable as your needs change.

* If you begin to read a book that is disappointing, don't feel compelled to finish it. You don't have time for uninspiring literature.

* If you are passionate about a project you are working on, stay focused; don't try to keep the house immaculate at the same time.

* Learn to let people help you do simple chores. They may not be able to get all of the spots out of the children's clothes, but the clothes will be clean.

* Accept that you have less-than-perfect relationships with some members of your family.

* Try not to get frustrated while learning a new skill. Practice will make you eventually do things with greater skill, ease, and pleasure.

* Do the hardest thing first and stick with it. Excellence builds over time.

Be happy you're pursuing an excellent life. Perfectionism is a bad dream that often ends in nightmares. Be glad the milk hasn't gone bad and that you are on a serious quest toward the good, not perfect, life. The good life is as good as life gets. Strive for no less or no more than this ideal.

> If a man aspires to the highest place, it is no dishonor to him
> to halt at the second, or even at the third.

CICERO

Get Organized

Good order is the foundation of all good things.

EDMUND BURKE

I still shudder at the memory of a naïve cleaning woman who rearranged all the books in my bookcase according to size and threw away a stack of newspaper clippings on my desk because she thought they looked messy. I was organized, but apparently I wasn't neat in her eyes. Living, as most of us have discovered, can look confused and untidy. Organization is key to a good life.

Because order precedes beauty, in my experience, we have to train ourselves to become organized in order to make the most of our lives. I read somewhere that the average executive wastes six weeks a year searching for lost files. For years my dear husband Peter made the living room of our Manhattan apartment his office. Every time we entertained, I would want to neaten things up. No matter what I did, it was disturbing to him to have his papers moved. "Things float. I don't know where anything is." No one could be more understanding than I was, because I feel the same way. My desk might look messy, but I know where my papers are. Eventually Peter moved his operation central to an office behind the kitchen, where he faces a picture window overlooking the East River with ample file drawers within arm's reach.

On a scale from one to ten, how organized do you think you are? How would you rate your spouse? How neat are you? Are you a minimalist, with a zero-sum rule? When something comes in, you get rid of something else? Do you tend to go overboard and be so conscientious about keeping things in order that you deny yourself and your family the fun of creative exploration? Do you allow your children to get dirty doing finger painting or other projects? Do you feel most comfortable having a lot of your favorite things around you in organized clutter? Is your home and office so cluttered, filled with things that get in your way, that you feel bogged down?

I love things. Lots of things. I'm a collector: I tend to save sweet letters and postcards. I'm careful about what I throw out. In fact, I find it painfully difficult to throw away anything that has some sentimental attachment. I never know when I'll want to go through drawers and be delighted by some surprise piece of memorabilia. Mihaly Csikszentmihalyi believes in order: "Taking care of one's home—throwing out the excess, redecorating to one's taste, making it personally and psychologically comfortable— could be the first step in reordering one's life."

The more organized you are, the more complex and interesting your life can become. If you set up systems with a place for everything, you can be relaxed and confident that you know where everything is and your life is not out of control or your house in disorder. I can't have any correspondence on my desk when I write. I either put letters on a desk different from the one where I'm working, or I put everything in a box with a lid, knowing that nothing will be disturbed until I have time to respond to letters. I've also learned to put all newspaper clippings I plan to read in a pretty folder so they, too, are safe.

When we analyze and organize our situation, we are less anxious, more peaceful and serene; we feel more efficient and in charge of our lives, able to do more with greater satisfaction and pleasure. If you try to strike a balance between saving everything and throwing away everything that's not nailed down, you can develop logical places to put things you and your family use, need, and enjoy.

When my interior design firm rented space from my husband Peter's law firm at 100 Park Avenue, there was one room that was time-shared; during the day it was used by my assistants and during the evening it was used by the law firm to do pro bono work. Every white Formica countertop had to be bare so there was no wasted time or confusion when they were put to a different use. This was a good discipline and doubled the usefulness of expensive real estate. The architect Buckminster Fuller would have been proud of us for conserving energy by using the space in the evening as well as during the day.

Greek author Nikos Kazantzakis lamented, "If only we, by weeping, laughing, and singing could create a law able to establish order over chaos!" It's easier to walk away and go dancing barefoot on a beach than to methodically label file folders, but both energies are necessary to living the good life. Kazantzakis wished he were more like his character Zorba and, perhaps, he was never able to strike a happy medium because of his serious commitment to his writing.

In my quest for order I've learned some helpful tools along the way. I hope they're useful to you. They seem so commonsense, but we are often blind to our own disorder.

* Keep the items you use every day nearest you. Things you use infrequently should be out of sight and should not take up living space.

* Try not to use your best spaces with light and view as storage areas. To open up space, store things in closets, not chests of drawers.

* For every separate project, have a separate file folder, even if only one document is in it.

* Avoid slush files and random stacks of papers. Immediately throw away junk mail as you go through your mail.

* Always put bills in an unpaid bill file, invitations in a "must respond" file, and letters you wish to keep in a box or a correspondence file.

* I'm a great believer in having portable files—some of mine are wicker boxes that house Pendiflex files, and others are accordion-type files with tabs that I can carry back and forth in a tote bag when I travel, so that I'm free to work on a variety of different and unrelated projects.

* Before beginning a project, great or small, put everything away, clear your desk of clutter. If your space is not a mess, it can be a moment's meditation to pay a bill or write a note.

* Try to make everything that is necessary and useful be as aesthetically pleasing as possible. If you can, have a flower or flowering plant in your workspace; it will remind you that everything you do well and with pleasure adds up to a good and beautiful life.

* Regularly weed out things that no longer function or are not used. Our needs change. Something that was once wonderful or necessary should not bog us down if we no longer require it. A notebook that doesn't lie flat is useless to me. Once you have fine-tuned your system, eliminate the things that aren't helpful. I use 4 x 6 file cards for my writing, for example, and carry 3 x 5 cards in my purse for my lists and notes of things to do. Any other size cards do not help me to remain organized.

* Keeping a running list of supplies so you never run out.

* Label and date everything—we think we'll remember, and we can't.

* Write everything down that you need to do. Keep your mind clear of clutter as you clear the clutter from your spaces.

* Build in time for children to tidy up their toys and puzzles and put their books back on the shelf.

The bigger your life, the more stuff you'll need to have. Be sure you find places that are convenient for your necessary and favorite things. Identify what your needs are as well as your desires. So many of the objects I enjoy having near me provide emotional comfort, adding greatly to my sense of well-being. Our possessions function in different ways—some are useful and practical while others are pretty and sentimental, feeding our soul. After your necessities are in place, surround yourself with meaningful objects that are deeply personal. If you love many things, you can find a place for them.

When you know where things are, when you have all the necessary parts fit into a functioning whole, you can embrace your life, take on more commitments, and do more creative work because you feel in charge, on top of things, up to the tasks and challenges. Think of all the things you want to accomplish. Begin now to get organized.

> Most of us believe in order to feel secure . . . to make our
> individual lives seem valuable and meaningful.

ALAN WATTS

Why Not Now?

It is eternity now. I am in the midst of it. It is about me in the sunshine; I am in it, as the butterfly in the light-laden air. Nothing has to come; it is now.
Now is eternity; now is the immortal life.

RICHARD JEFFRIES

Here we are. Now we can commit ourselves to living by the Golden Triangle of the three most challenging words: *true, good,* and *beautiful.* We live in a great world full of excitement. Now is all you and I have; we should go for the good life. I have a friend who saw a sign at Massachusetts General Hospital: "Yesterday is gone, tomorrow is a mystery. Now is a gift. That is why we call it the *present.*"

Accept the invitation. Live your philosophy and apply the ideals of life to every choice you make. There is a great potential in you waiting to unfold. Contemplate the joys of being alive. Embrace the depth of your living. We live in eternity now. We must wake up to the truth that this hour, this day's delight, is eternity. There is no there *there*, eternity is here, now. We must say yes to accepting this great gift we have right where we are. Right here, right now, we live the good life. When we realize how vitally important now really is to us, we can join all the great minds through philosophy, literature, poetry, religion, music, and art, who show us that great lives are possible. Now we must transform ourselves. Not only should we commit ourselves to all that is true, good, and beautiful, as a way to live in the light of excellence, in the joy of natural beauty, but we should put our whole being into now.

The Buddha reminds us, "Life is as fleeting as a rainbow, a flash of lightning, a star at dawn." Whatever your beliefs about what happens after we die, don't think you can put your life on hold, waiting to live the good life later. There is no way we can delay our challenging journey toward a life of real excellence and meaning. As the poet Emily Dickinson believed, "That it will never come again is what makes life so sweet." We can't afford to shortchange ourselves.

Goethe brilliantly instructed us to "Live in this moment and live in eternity." This genius who was continuously alive to the transcendent experience, along with so many other great minds, urges us to enjoy now, to live more abundantly. On his deathbed, he said, "Light—more light." We're given this life, this tiny window of light, of opportunity. Don't think of now as a good time. Know that now is the only time.

The good life, the well-lived life, the one life you are now living, is yours. You have a duty and obligation to make it happy by living by the principles of the moderate mean between two extremes of too little or too much. You need to continuously challenge yourself to move in a transcendent direction. If you are financially comfortable and secure, you may choose to give more money to worthy causes in order to help others live better lives. To live in the middle, between too little and too much, is your challenge because this is the right place for our greatest good.

You are your choices. You live with the consequences for better or for worse. Is there a better way of life for you and me? The task for us is to learn how to think in an entirely new way. Without training our minds, we will not be able to make the good, the better, and the best choices. The Buddha believed, "Each morning we are born again." You and I can create the ideal way to live right where we are by living the good life now. In our positive thoughts, our constructive attitudes, our right choices, our thoughtful actions, in our capacity to grow in love, we are able to live in the light of truth now.

Do whatever it takes to make now more precious. The most ordinary experience can become extraordinary with the right mental discipline and the gift of our life-giving force. We recognize how blessed we are. We're grateful for our life. We appreciate what we have before it is too late.

Studies prove that when people are more mature, they tend to be happier. They're less emotionally imbalanced and have a tendency to savor what they have now. There are no guarantees that any of us will live long, healthy lives. Now is the time we should choose to make sublime. My mentor and friend Eleanor McMillen Brown, the doyenne of interior design in America, lived a life of great excellence. I've never known anyone more balanced, disciplined, talented, and charming. She understood that all beauty warms our heart. Her generosity of spirit, her tenderness, her cheerfulness, were inspiring. Her heart was always in the right place. She taught the good life by example.

Mrs. Brown's favorite word was success. I wish you could hear her: "Oh, Sandie, that was such a S-U-C-C-E-S-S!" It could have been a Thanksgiving dinner or a room scheme or a wonderful luncheon together. This was a lady who loved life, who wanted things to work out well. Mrs. Brown set a high standard of excellence for me to try to follow. She understood that everything could be true, good, and beautiful and lived this philosophy every day. We set ourselves up for success when we recognize that everything we do is important. We can't live well in parts. We live a happy, productive, beautiful life in everything we choose to do.

I look to the central figure of American transcendentalism, Emerson, for inspiration: "How high can you carry life? A man is a man only as he makes life and nature happier to us."

"How high can you carry life?" Commit yourself to living the good life. Accept the invitation. Find pleasure in the process of transcendence into greater truth, goodness, and beauty. Now or never. Now is when we're free to choose to affirm life more fully, to embrace excellence.

Living the good life is challenging. The commitment to live such a life will not make life easier. But when we understand that the good life is the one right way for each of us to live, we can gladly accept the invitation. Now we are on our way, headed in the right direction. Guided by the principles that will light our path, we can choose to live the good life. Now we have everything we need and desire. Nothing is missing. Everything is eternally and forever now. This is IT. We are *now* in the sunshine. If not now, when?

> The one fact that I would cry from every housetop is this: The good life is waiting for us—here and now! At this very moment we have the necessary techniques, both material and psychological, to create a full and satisfying life for everyone.
>
> **B. F. SKINNER**

Wise Choices, Yes, and Good Luck

Recognize the value of each additional moment, and receive it as though it happened by wonderful, incredible luck.

PHILODEMUS

Twenty-five centuries ago, the great Greek thinker Aristotle was known for his uncommon common sense. His wisdom helps us understand our own lives, our real world, and our society. His great insights and understanding are not at all common. Aristotle understood that our success in living the good life depends on moral virtue or excellence due to our good, wise choices, the right choices we make every day that are aimed at what is good for us.

But that's not enough. We can make a great effort to live a good life, but if we have bad luck, we will not be able to have all the external good we'll need to live a good life. We didn't have any control over the circumstances of our birth, our parents, or where and how we were raised. We cannot will good luck by making wise choices.

Think of the earthquake that spawned the tsunami, or of recent hurricanes of horror and unbearable destruction. Even when we try to take good care of our body, there is no guarantee we will maintain our health and vitality. Disease happens to us, our family and our friends, not by choice. Health and prosperity, to some extent, are due to luck smiling on us. Some people are extremely blessed with good luck, while others are unfortunate, having to endure one misfortune after another. The real goods we need to live a good life, then, are not entirely within our power to obtain by our wise choices.

Carl Brandt told me over a memorable lunch meeting that I have been blessed with good luck. He recognizes that I work hard, but many others do also, and don't feel happy or meet with success. He's absolutely right. Fortuitous circumstances have brought me great good luck. I've been extremely fortunate all of my life. If I'd been born male, chances are I would not have been taken around the world by my aunt, Betty Johns. She wisely chose to take her three oldest nieces, not her nephews. My father didn't believe women should receive the same education as men, but this world trip profoundly changed me in a far more dramatic and meaningful way than could be imagined in a school setting.

While we can't make good luck, we can take notice of it when we are blessed by good fortune. Good luck is a gift. Chance, the unpredictable element of existence, does play a major role in all of our lives, for good and for bad. We should recognize the need for good luck as well as wise choices when we're pursuing happiness. Take heart. Your determination to make good choices, in the good and bad circumstances of your life, will fortify your inner resolve, mobilize your resources, and help you to grow through, not merely go through, misfortune. Our habits of choice help us in good and bad times. Saint Catherine of Siena said, "To a brave man, good and bad luck are like his right and left hand. He uses both."

Aristotle believed that trying to live a good life is worth all the trouble and effort it takes. He freely admitted it is not easy to live up to his high principles. But every time we make the right choice and follow it through, we move toward our ultimate goal of living a happy life. The nineteenth-century French chemist Louis Pasteur, who founded modern microbiology and invented pasteurization, believed, "Chance favors the prepared mind." Someone once said that the harder you work, the more luck you have.

Do not feel the aim and goal of happiness is selfish, only for your own good life. No one succeeds in achieving happiness without considering the well-being and happiness of others. Through our love of life, our love of ourselves, and our love of others, we'll want to play our part to add to the universal intelligence, order, and wisdom.

We should look at our life as a whole. The big picture requires that we take whatever pains are required to live a good life. We need to stretch our intellectual capacities in order to achieve excellence. Acquiring knowledge and developing our skills can be painful, but it is what's good for us and others in the long run.

We're extremely fortunate to have freedom of choice. If we ever doubt this, we just need to look around us. We alone choose. As we know, choices aren't always sweet. If we have bad fortune, we have to make the wisest choice under awful circumstances. But whenever we're willing to face each choice with integrity and conviction, we will be exercising our fundamental responsibility as the highest species, as thinking human beings. As humans, we have a hunger and thirst to know, to learn, and to challenge ourselves, to make real use of our abilities by developing our innate potential, our unique gifts.

We have free will to shape and mold ourselves into a superior life. We can't afford to be afraid to carve out a real life for ourselves, not one that others choose for us. We are the embodiment of our choices. We should try to take the high road. Happiness and the good life are possible when we strive for excellence, when we try to be reasonable and fair, when we exercise our higher powers, when we try to live in the transcendent consciousness of love.

Your unique personality, temperament, disposition, and outlook on life will guide you. You have everything you will need right now, right where you are. Remember that the pleasures of the mind are unlimited. You're always better off the more knowledge you have. You now have a solid plan for the good life. There are no certainties, no promises; only possibilities and probabilities. You can't control what happens to you by chance, but you can increase your chances of good luck when you are prepared. Take full advantage of all the good things that come to you.

When you face bad fortune, try to lessen the impact of the blow, to bring your life back into balance. Fortitude is an essential ingredient in a successful life. When we have the ability to endure through strength of mind, this character trait allows us to suffer pain and adversity with strength, courage, and perseverance.

I hope these fifty ways to live the good life help guide your course. Always know that you have access to the wisdom of the universe inside you, available whenever you tap into this deep resource. You are pure potential and are endowed with the ability to handle situations well. The good life is boundless in opportunities, in excitement, fun, pleasure, and excellence. When you commit yourself to living on this right path, the universe and its fundamental laws will support and uplift you.

You are truly on your way. Choice by choice, you will be directing all your energies toward an extraordinarily rich and meaningful life. Choose to live the good life with your whole heart. Wisdom will support you every step of the way. I wish you great happiness and good luck.

> Wisdom—meaning judgment—acting on experience, common sense,
> available knowledge, and a decent appreciation of probability.
>
> **BARBARA W. TUCHMAN**

LET
ALEXANDRA STODDARD
INSPIRE YOUR LIFE

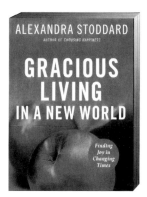
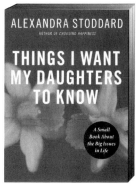

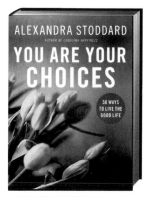